REVIEWS FOR

The First 30 Days

You may have picked up this book in a place of brokenness, emptiness, or regret. Or, perhaps you chose this book in hopes of finding a deeper intimacy with God. However, this book ended up in your hands, I assure you that you will feel the impact well beyond the thirty days.

As you journey through this book, you will find that Katina writes from the real and raw experiences of life and faith. Her words have a genuineness and depth because before the pen hit the page she had experienced it herself. Katina's transparency will remind everyone that despite what has happened to you, God in His great mercy, can work all things together for good.

It's hard to find people who will not only celebrate the victories with you, but also walk through the valley with you. Katina has not only held my hand through the valley, but she has done the same for so many others. I pray that you feel the same faith, love, and hope that I felt as she journeyed with me.

No matter what season of life you're in, I am expectant that God will do a new work in you as you read this book.

—**Emma Hoffman**, Youth Pastor.

***

Your view of life depends on the lens you are looking through. Katina Wetter's 30-day devotional is like an eye exam using a Biblical lens that will dramatically transform your outlook on life and eternity.

—**Gary Varvel**, nationally syndicated cartoonist.

***

This book is REAL. This is NOT a teaching to help us create the appearance of a perfect life on social media. Katina uses real stories; as raw and dark as some of them are, to help us address the very real and present dark areas in each one of us. Her transparency and honesty are refreshing. This 30-day journey will cause the reader to explore deep within themselves to deal with doubts, sins, hurts, issues, and even some of the deepest and darkest pains of human existence. So many Christians live Sunday to Sunday putting their church faces on while suffering inside or living a shallow faith that looks great on social media but will stand very weak before the Living God.

Although the title implies 30 days, I believe you will begin to see transformation the first week. And I believe the results you gain will last well beyond 30 days, standing the test of time for all of eternity. I add my faith to your faith that your destiny is being revolutionized through applying the teachings of this book.

—**Pastor Matt Nichols,** Founder of *Matt Nichols Ministry*.

***

The First 30 Days offered encouragement and empowered me to always follow the Christian faith. I feel like a stronger person towards God and my church. All of us face crises in life, and these personal stories by Katina will help us all on our spiritual journey and will offer hope to everyone. Katina's stories will encourage and inspire readers to stay on course with God for years to come.

—**Susan Fagg**, Kindergarten Teacher.

***

If you are looking for a fresh perspective on life or if you are seeking a renewed heart or a revitalized spiritual life, you've come to the right place. Through honesty, vulnerability and a firm grace, Katina gently walks the reader through her own broken experiences and helps the reader find healing for their own brokenness. The focus on Scripture in this book is paramount and refreshing, and the journal prompts are powerful and effective in helping us transform to look more like Jesus!

—**Shannon Carroll**, Co-Author of the #1 Best-selling book, "*One Thing Remains.*"

***

You have done your research and everything is very clear and concise.

I appreciate all the direction given daily and the questions.

The verses to ponder made me feel connected to God's Word. I couldn't wait to search in the bible.

Well done.

—**Di Carter**, Co-Founder *of Nonprofit Faith Based at Christ fest Pc & Mrs. Indiana 2020 at Women of Achievement.*

The First 30 Days

A Challenge to Change Your Mind and Revolutionize Your Eternal Destiny

Katina Wetter-Wright

Published by KHARIS PUBLISHING, imprint of KHARIS MEDIA LLC.

Copyright © 2021 Katina Wetter-Wright

ISBN-13: 978-1-63746-024-5
ISBN-10: 1-63746-024-4

Library of Congress Control Number: 2021932063

All rights reserved. This book or parts thereof may not be reproduced in any form, stored in a retrieval system, or transmitted in any form by any means - electronic, mechanical, photocopy, recording, or otherwise - without prior written permission of the publisher, except as provided by United States of America copyright law.

All Scripture quotations, unless otherwise indicated, are taken from the Holy Bible, New International Version®, NIV®. Copyright ©1973, 1978, 1984, 2011 by Biblical, Inc.™ Used by permission.

All KHARIS PUBLISHING products are available at special quantity discounts for bulk purchase for sales promotions, premiums, fund-raising, and educational needs. For details, contact:

Kharis Media LLC
Tel: 1-479-599-8657
support@kharispublishing.com
www.kharispublishing.com

TABLE OF CONTENTS

	The Challenge	ix
1	Where Do I Begin?	1
2	How Do I See My Life?	5
3	How Am I Affected?	8
4	So, Who Is God?	12
5	Who Is God the Father?	16
6	What Makes a Loving Father?	19
7	What Is Compassion?	23
8	What Is Honesty?	27
9	Who Is Your Protector?	30
10	What Are Your Needs?	35
11	Who Are You in Relationship With?	39
12	Why Discipline?	43
13	Who Is Your Role Model?	48
14	What Is a Legacy?	52
15	What Do You Choose?	56
16	Are You Deceived?	59
17	What Are Your Hardships?	64

18	Do You Doubt?	68
19	What Is Power?	73
20	Where Do You Get Your Power?	77
21	What is Faith?	80
22	Is Your Faith Hindered?	84
23	How Do You Activate Faith?	87
24	Who Are You Waiting For?	91
25	How Do You Increase Faith?	94
26	Do You Exercise Your Faith?	97
27	What Are You Promised?	101
28	How Do You View Faith?	105
29	Who Will Never Leave?	110
30	Are You Living Successfully?	114
	Eternal Choices	120
	New Book coming soon…	125
	Bibliography	128

The Challenge

Maybe you're reading this book and you think I am a QUACK! Great! Give me 30 days to change your mind.

Maybe you picked up this book, and you know Jesus. Great! Take this journey and fall more in love with Him.

It's possible you're someplace in-between thinking I'm a QUACK and being a Jesus lover. Great! Sticking with me for 30 days can change your life, too.

What do you have to lose?

Today, I am challenging you to take a 30-day journey. For 30 days, you will read, discuss, and ponder the things of God. You will take 30 days to get to know Jesus. All I ask is that during these 30 days you will be faithful and you will challenge yourself to think and learn with an open mind.

My personal prayer is that, at the end of these 30 days, you will make a commitment or reaffirmation to Jesus that will change your life and seal your eternal home.

"For there is no difference between Jew and Gentile-- the same Lord is Lord of all and richly blesses all who call on him, for, "Everyone who calls on the name of the Lord will be saved.'" Romans 10:12-13 NIV

Attention: If you need more space to complete the study guide pages in this book, you can find a downloadable file at:
www.reflectionsofabeliever.org. or via google drive at:
https://drive.google.com/file/d/1yUrTO_yMsDWteBNe_-KsAbVcnooA5lWM/view?usp=sharing

Day 1

Where Do I Begin?

BEFORE READING	AFTER READING
Why did you pick up this book?	What do you hope to accomplish in the next 30 days?
Before reading, I feel...	After reading, I feel...
What are the first three words you think of when I mention God?	What stood out to you the most in today's reading? Can you make a true, unbiased commitment from this point on?

Introduction

What defines how you see yourself? How do you determine your own self-worth?

Many of us pride ourselves on our families, our work, the size of our bank account, our toys, our popularity, and yes, even our bodies. We look to the world around us and judge who we are or who we want to be according to another person's successes or failures. This is because many of us gain our own self-worth through the eyes of this world.

See, as humans, we have an innate desire to belong, to be loved, to connect. We need connections and we will find them in one place or another. Some connections are good and some are bad, but no matter where you are in life, no matter what connections you have made, there is always room for growth.

The Bible tells us in 2 Corinthians 3:18 NKJV we are being "transformed from glory to glory," meaning we are continually changing and growing. Yet the truth is, each day we are changing either for God or for ourselves. We can change and grow in a positive way, from "glory to glory," or we can change and grow in a worldly way.

I have witnessed many people I know and love turn to the things of this world, only to be disappointed and ruin their lives. They run from the idea of God because of the hurts and pain of this world. The truth is, true fulfillment does not come from worldly possessions or praises, it comes from a relationship with God.

This book is designed in such a way that you can complete it on your own or with others. Whichever option you choose, it is up to you how much you get out of the experience. As you work through this book, you will be asked some tough questions. Be honest. Sometimes, before you can heal a deep wound, the wound must first be exposed.

From this point on, before each day's readings, you will see a questionnaire. The **left side** is to be completed **before your reading**. (I do often break the I Am Thinking, and I Am Feeling sections into a before and after, but that is up to you.) The **right side** is to be completed **after your reading**. If you are working with a group, discuss your answers. If you would like to participate in an online group discussion, go to Reflections of a Believer Facebook Page. Or www.reflectionsofabeliever.org

From this point forward, you are in control.

Verses to Ponder:

But we all, with unveiled face, beholding as in a mirror the glory of the Lord, are being transformed into the same image from glory to glory, just as by the Spirit of the Lord. 2 Corinthians 3:18 NKJV

For everything in the world—the lust of the flesh, the lust of the eyes, and the pride of life—comes not from the Father but from the world. The world and its desires pass away, but whoever does the will of God lives forever. 1 John 2:16-17 NIV

There is a way that appears to be right, but in the end it leads to death. Proverbs 14:12 NIV

'For I know the plans I have for you,' declares the Lord, 'plans to prosper you and not to harm you, plans to give you hope and a future.' Jeremiah 29:11 NIV

For we are God's handiwork, created in Christ Jesus to do good works, which God prepared in advance for us to do. Ephesians 2:10 NIV

Day 2

How Do I See My Life?

BEFORE READING | AFTER READING

What has been your greatest hurt in life?

How do you feel your perception of life effects your ability to depend on God?

Before reading, I feel...

After reading, I feel...

When you think of your life as a whole, what experiences have shaped how you view life?

What patterns in life have you fallen back into?

What price have you paid for those patterns?

Looking Inward

Each person has grown up with a different set of experiences. You can live in the same house, experience the same joys, trials, and moments in time, and still view life in entirely different ways from those who grew up there, too.

See, each of us looks at life through our own unique life lens. This lens determines so much about us. It determines if we are pessimistic or optimistic. It determines if we are a go-getter or a go to the couch-er.

In fact, the way we view life largely determines what experiences we will have and how those experiences will play out in our lives.

Let me give an example: As a young girl, I was molested. This violation prompted and manifested emotions in me that I did not understand. I was scarred, lost and broken for many years, jumping from one long-term relationship to the next, searching for someone to fill a void within me.

Being scarred, I never felt good enough. I was always second-guessing myself. Whenever anything went wrong in a relationship, I assumed I had caused it. Now, looking back, I realize many of the issues were not from me, but from my inability to stand up for myself, my inability to realize my own self-worth.

You see, I had allowed an experience to mar my perception of life, how I should be treated, and how I should act. Therefore, I repeated the same cycles over and over for a large portion of my youth.

It wasn't until I really began to depend on God that my perception of life began to shift. Even though I knew of

God when I was younger, I did not **know** God. I did not have a genuine relationship with Him.

Throughout the next few entries, we will explore who God really is. Sit back, hold on, and enjoy the ride.

Verses to Ponder:

The wise person has his eyes in his head, but the fool walks in darkness. And yet I perceived that the same event happens to all of them. Ecclesiastes 2:14 ESV

He sees many things, but does not observe them; his ears are open, but he does not hear. Isaiah 42:20 ESV

And Jesus, aware of this, said to them, 'Why are you discussing the fact that you have no bread? Do you not yet perceive or understand? Are your hearts hardened? Having eyes do you not see, and having ears do you not hear? And do you not remember?' Mark 8:17-18 ESV

The way of a fool is right in his own eyes, but a wise man listens to advice. Proverbs 12:15 ESV

Trust in the LORD with all your heart, and do not lean on your own understanding. Proverbs 3:5 ESV

Why do you see the speck that is in your brother's eye, but do not notice the log that is in your own eye? Matthew 7:3 ESV

For God speaks in one way, and in two, though man does not perceive it. Job 33:14 ESV

Day 3

How Am I Affected?

BEFORE READING | **AFTER READING**

How do the patterns you fall back into, affect your life positively or negatively?	After reading today, what patterns would you like to work on to improve your life?
Before reading, I feel…	After reading, I feel…
What are 1-4 patterns you would like to see in your life?	Before reading, you were asked to write 1-4 patterns you would like to see in your life. What can you do to accomplish these patterns? How can God help you through this process?

Patterns

How do the patterns you fall back into, affect your life?

Now, that is a hard question. As I look back over my life, I can say some patterns I have fallen back into have been great. I have three undergraduate and graduate degrees because I love to learn.

On the other hand, some patterns have made my life much harder than it had to be. For example, my search to feel loved and accepted led me to many bad relationship choices.

One particular relationship was very toxic. Although this man was never physically abusive, his mental abuse and manipulation were detrimental to me. As much as I would like to say it was all his fault, it was not. I had gotten myself into a pattern of picking men I thought I could save, men I felt could fill a void inside me. It was a void I later learned could only be filled by Jesus.

Many times in my life, I did not even realize how truly broken I was. I did not realize I was picking a different man with the same characteristics, only to relive the same turbulent relationship with the same end results.

We all have patterns in our lives that we tend to fall back on, some small, some not so small. For some people, it may be drugs, alcohol, sex, gossiping, food, toxic relationships, or any number of behaviors that affect our lives. We tend to fall back into these patterns because they are known. They are safe to our way of life, the life we are used to.

Sometimes, to see how genuinely detrimental these

habits and patterns are to our lives, we need to take a step back and look at their effects on us. What is the ultimate cost of these choices? Do they cost us time with our families? Do they cost us money we could use elsewhere? Do they cost us our health? What are the real costs of these habits?

For me, the highest price I paid was my own self-worth. I look back and see how many of my choices were intertwined. I clearly see how my life choices became a beast of my own creation. One bad decision led to another and another until God pulled me from a pit of my own creation and set me on solid ground.

Verses to Ponder:

Since therefore the children share in flesh and blood, he himself likewise partook of the same things, that through death he might destroy the one who has the power of death, that is, the devil, and deliver all those who through fear of death were subject to lifelong slavery. Hebrews 2: 14-15 ESV

May you be strengthened with all power, according to his glorious might, for all endurance and patience with joy, giving thanks to the Father, who has qualified you to share in the inheritance of the saints in light. He has delivered us from the domain of darkness and transferred us to the kingdom of his beloved Son, in whom we have redemption, the forgiveness of sins. Colossians 1:11-14 HCSB

For I will be merciful toward their iniquities, and I will

The First 30 Days

remember their sins no more. Hebrews 8:12 ESV

For God so loved the world, that he gave his only Son, that whoever believes in him should not perish but have eternal life. For God did not send his Son into the world to condemn the world, but in order that the world might be saved through him. John 3:16-17 ESV

For I will be merciful toward their iniquities, and I will remember their sins no more. Hebrews 8:12 ESV

Day 4

So, Who Is God?

BEFORE READING **AFTER READING**

Right now, how do you view God?

What hurts do you blame on God?

Before reading, I feel...

After reading, I feel...

What do you have a hard time letting go control of?

How do you feel and what do you think about the statement, "A good God would not allow bad things to happen?"

The First 30 Days

Who is God?: Introduction

Many people view God as this mythical man in the sky, as someone who, if real, would shoot lightning bolts down on unsuspecting victims. They have a hard time believing He exists because they cannot touch Him or see Him in the physical realm. The truth is, "God is spirit," according to John 4:24 NIV. He is not confined to one place or one person. He is omnipresent and omnipotent. Proverbs 15:3 ESV says it like this: "The eyes of the Lord are in everyplace, keeping watch on the evil and the good."

People have a hard time understanding how God can be omnipresent and omnipotent, therefore, they deny His presence all together. Much of this denial is rooted in an inability to look outside of themselves. To trust in God, you have to be able to let go of your own control. You have to understand, although you call the shots, God has a good plan for you to walk in, if only you will walk the path He has laid out for you. Although this path will not always be a bed of roses, it will produce a successful life if you stick with it.

The Bible tells us in Jeremiah 29:11 NIV, "For I know the plans I have for you," declares the LORD, "plans to prosper you and not to harm you, plans to give you hope and a future."

Unfortunately, in many instances, when a person is hurting, they turn from the idea of God because "a good God would not allow bad things to happen." Then, instead of confronting God with their pain and hurt, they simply walk away from God's plan for their life.

Over the next few weeks, we are going to look at the character of God. During this time, I ask that you look at God from an open and objective stance. Lay down any preconceived notions you may have about who God is or who He isn't. Just lean into the scriptures and take Him in.

Verses to Ponder:

God is spirit, and those who worship him must worship in spirit and truth. John 4:24 ESV

Jesus said to him, "I am the way, and the truth, and the life. No one comes to the Father except through me. John 14:6 ESV

I am the Alpha and the Omega, the First and the Last, the Beginning and the End. Revelation 22:13 NLT

The Rock, his work is perfect, for all his ways are justice. A God of faithfulness and without iniquity, just and upright is he. Deuteronomy 32:4 ESV

In hope of eternal life, which God, who never lies, promised before the ages began. Titus 1:2 ESV

For by him all things were created, in heaven and on earth, visible and invisible, whether thrones or dominions or rulers or authorities—all things were created through him and for him. Colossians 1:16 ESV

In the beginning, God created the heavens and the earth. Genesis 1:1 ESV

To the King of ages, immortal, invisible, the only God, be honor and glory forever and ever. Amen. 1 Timothy 1:17 ESV

God said to Moses, 'I AM WHO I AM.' And he said, 'Say this to the people of Israel, I AM has sent me to you.' Exodus 3:14 ESV

The First 30 Days

"In the beginning was the Word, and the Word was with God, and the Word was God." John 1:1 ESV

Day 5

Who Is God the Father?

BEFORE READING

What do you think of when you picture the perfect father?

Before reading, I feel...

List three things that describe your father?

AFTER READING

After today's reading, do you believe God possesses the qualities mentioned? Why or why not?

After reading, I feel...

How do you feel your father has influenced your idea of God?

What attributes from my list or your own do you feel are the essential attributes for God to possess?

God the Father

To understand the nature of God, you must understand who He is. God is our Heavenly Father. Did you catch that? He is our father. Second Corinthians 6:18 NKJV says, "I will be a Father to you, and you shall be My sons and daughters, Says the Lord Almighty."

Now, for some, it can be hard to relate to God the Father because your idea of a father has been skewed by a worldly father who was less than what you expected him to be. As mentioned earlier, our life lens can alter our view of our experiences. No matter what our natural father was like, good or bad, God is so much more than any man could ever be.

This is not to put a good father down; no, good fathers deserve praise. But every father, good or bad, makes mistakes. God, on the other hand, is the perfect example of fatherhood. The Bible tells us in Numbers 23:19 NIV, "God is not human, that he should lie, not a human being, that he should change his mind. Does he speak and then not act? Does he promise and not fulfill?"

This verse goes straight to the character of God. First, God cannot lie. He is Holy, and within the pages of His Holy Word, you find truths about His character, His love for you, parenting, life, and so much more.

That said, since God is truth and He cannot lie, He must exhibit all the attributes of the perfect father: loving, compassionate, honest, protective, legacy-leaving, a good role model, one who meets needs, a disciplinarian, and relationship-seeking. We will explore these attributes over the next few days. Enjoy getting to know the great I AM.

Verses to Ponder:

*To our God and Father be glory for ever and ever.
Amen.* Philippians 4:20 NIV

Are not two sparrows sold for a penny? Yet not one of them will fall to the ground outside your Father's care. And even the very hairs of your head are all numbered. So don't be afraid; you are worth more than many sparrows. Matthew 10:29-31 NIV

yet for us there is but one God, the Father, from whom all things came and for whom we live; and there is but one Lord, Jesus Christ, through whom all things came and through whom we live.
1 Corinthians 8:6 NIV

Day 6

What Makes a Loving Father?

God's Love

Love is a word we humans use often. I love sugar cream pie. I love Maine. I love my family. I would venture to say that the way I love sugar cream pie is not the same way that I love my family. If it is, I am in big trouble.

See, as humans, we use the word "love" to describe so many different forms of affection. In fact, we use it so much that the word has been muddied-down over time. True love, or should I say, Biblical love, is not something that you fall into and out of as fast as you change your clothes. No, Biblical love is something that you work at, something you sacrifice for. Biblical love means putting someone else ahead of yourself, no matter the cost.

God is the ultimate picture of Biblical love. First John 4:9-10 NIV says, "This is how God showed his love among us: He sent his one and only Son into the world that we might live through him. This is love: not that we loved God, but that he loved us and sent his Son as an atoning sacrifice for our sins."

Many people may ask how this shows love. Imagine being a parent and knowing that the only way you can save someone is to allow your perfectly healthy child to be an organ donor. I can honestly say I wouldn't do it. God, on the other hand, knew that the only way to save the human race was to watch His only child suffer. He knew that although there would be pain and suffering, Jesus would be the ultimate example of love, sacrifice, honesty, and so much more. God knew by the shedding of His perfect blood, Jesus would wash us white as snow.

See, love is not about what we can get. It is about what

we can give, regardless of what we receive in return. God understands that we are imperfect. He forgives us even when we do not deserve it. Isaiah 43:25 NIV says, "I, even I, am he who blots out your transgressions, for my own sake, and remembers your sins no more."

No matter what we do, God loves us so much that He will forgive us. In fact, He loves us so much that He made the way for us to be atoned from our sins. He gave us His only Son as an example, as a brother, as the perfect redemptive sacrifice. The only thing that He asks in return is that we love others the way He loves us and follow His example of Biblical love. John 15:12-13 NIV says, "My command is this: Love each other as I have loved you. Greater love has no one than this: to lay down one's life for one's friends."

This type of love is getting harder and harder to find, therefore, it is becoming increasingly harder to comprehend the true magnitude of love that God has for His children. It isn't until we truly understand who God is that we will be able to comprehend how much He truly loves us.

Verses to Ponder:

They refused to listen and failed to remember the miracles you performed among them. They became stiff-necked and in their rebellion appointed a leader in order to return to their slavery. But you are a forgiving God, gracious and compassionate, slow to anger and abounding in love. Therefore you did not desert them.
Nehemiah 9:17 NIV

> *'Though the mountains be shaken*
> *and the hills be removed,*
> *yet my unfailing love for you will not be shaken*
> *nor my covenant of peace be removed,'*
> *says the LORD, who has compassion on you.*
> Isaiah 54:10 NIV

> *But now, this is what the LORD says—*
> *he who created you, Jacob,*
> *he who formed you, Israel:*
> *'Do not fear, for I have redeemed you;*
> *I have summoned you by name; you are mine.*
> *When you pass through the waters,*
> *I will be with you;*
> *and when you pass through the rivers,*
> *they will not sweep over you.*
> *When you walk through the fire,*
> *you will not be burned;*
> *the flames will not set you ablaze.*
> *For I am the LORD your God,*
> *the Holy One of Israel, your Savior;*
> *I give Egypt for your ransom,*
> *Cush[a] and Seba in your stead.'*
> Isaiah 43:1-3 NIV

Day 7

What Is Compassion?

BEFORE READING	AFTER READING
When have you shown compassion to another person?	Look back over your life and list a time that you were protected from something.
Before reading, I feel...	After reading, I feel...
List three words you feel describe compassion.	After reading, have your ideas on compassion shifted? How can you show Godly compassion to others?

True Compassion

Compassion is a trait that seems to be lacking in society today. Many people are so caught up in what they want, what makes them feel good, that they forget to see how their actions affect others. There is a "me first" mentality that has become mainstream, causing compassion for others to fall to the wayside.

So, what is compassion? Webster's dictionary defines compassion as, "sympathetic consciousness of others' distress together with a desire to alleviate it."

See, compassion is not just seeing that someone is hurting, it is wanting to do something to help them through the pain. There are many instances in the Bible where God's people are in pain. In many of those instances, their pain was caused by their own disobedience.

Regardless of the cause, God showed compassion to His children. You'll see one of the first instances of compassion in Exodus 32. In this chapter, the Israelites have been saved from the harsh treatment of the pharaoh by God through His use of Moses and Aaron. Moses had retreated to Mount Sinai to receive instructions from God. At the beginning of Chapter 32, you see the people are growing restless. With their leader gone, they begin to stray and demand Aaron to make a golden calf for them to worship.

Now, to get the full picture, you must understand what God had delivered them from. The Israelites had been slaves in Egypt, oppressed, downtrodden, and mistreated. The pharaoh had commanded their baby boys to be forcibly taken and murdered to curb population growth. (Exodus 1:15-16 ESV)

Then God delivered them out of the land where they were being mistreated, asking only that they trust in Him. Instead, they demanded a false god be erected to go before them. Not only that, but they sacrificed and bowed down to the idol, claiming it had delivered them from the hands of the pharaoh. (Exodus 32:1 NIV, Exodus 32:6-8 NIV) This was the ultimate act of betrayal for a people who had been given direct instruction from God not to erect false gods (Exodus 20:22 NIV). The wages of this sin was death.

God's anger burned against the Israelites in Exodus 32:7-10 NIV, but Moses interceded for them in verses 11-13 NIV. He pleaded with God to not wipe out the entire Israelite population. In an act of compassion, God relented. The Bible says it like this in Exodus 32:14 NIV, "Then the LORD relented and did not bring on his people the disaster he had threatened." God would have been justified in wiping out the entire population, but He showed compassion on them instead.

See, although God was stern, He loved His children and showed them compassion even when they turned from Him. Likewise, God shows us compassion, even when we are not walking with Him. One such example from my life was during college.

I was not walking with God. I knew of Him. I even went to church occasionally, but I did not walk with Him during my first year of college. In fact, I was living up my freedom. One day, I decided to get on the back of a motorcycle with a guy. Twenty minutes later, I was broken, bruised, my body wrapped around a tree.

Later, the ambulance driver told me that when he arrived I wasn't breathing. As he worked on me, some ladies from a church next to the accident site started to pray over me and my then-boyfriend. In an act of compassion, although I was far from God, He spared my life.

I wish I could say I was perfect from that point on, but I have not been. In spite of my imperfections, God has continued to show compassion to me. The Bible tells us in 2 Peter 3:9 NIV, "The Lord is not slow in keeping his promise, as some understand slowness. Instead, he is patient with you, not wanting anyone to perish, but everyone to come to repentance."

In His compassion for us, He gives us every opportunity to get our lives right. He will protect us even when we are being ignorant.

Verses to Ponder:

But you, O Lord, are a God merciful and gracious, slow to anger and abounding in steadfast love and faithfulness. Psalm 86:15 ESV

Therefore the LORD waits to be gracious to you, and therefore he exalts himself to show mercy to you. For the LORD is a God of justice; blessed are all those who wait for him. Isaiah 30:18 ESV

Have mercy on me, O God, according to your steadfast love; according to your abundant mercy blot out my transgressions. Psalm 51:1 ESV

The steadfast love of the LORD never ceases; his mercies never come to an end; they are new every morning; great is your faithfulness. Lamentations 3:22-23 ESV

Day 8

What Is Honesty?

BEFORE READING | **AFTER READING**

What is honesty?

Is it hard for you to comprehend a God who is perfect and never lies? Why or why not?

Before reading, I feel...

After reading, I feel...

When you think of your life as a whole, what experiences have shaped how you view your life?

Honesty can be hard at times. What are some ways you struggle with honesty?

What are you willing to do to become more honest?

Honesty

Honesty is the best policy. I am sure everyone has heard that old saying sometime in their life. As accurate as this statement is, there are times when it can be hard to be honest... times when we don't want to hurt someone's feelings, times when we want to manipulate a situation, or even times when we just flat out don't want to get in trouble.

Many people, Christian and Non-Christian's alike, are unreliable. They say one thing and do another. We say we will do something, but we bail because something else comes up. We make a commitment or a promise, but then we rationalize in our mind why we cannot do what we said.

My pastor has often said, "Let your yes mean yes, and your no mean no!" (Matthew 5:37 NKJV) Unfortunately, unless we commit to doing what we say, regardless of the sacrifice we must make, we will likely find ourselves in situations where we lie, as unintentionally as it may be.

Whatever the reason we lie, there are times, as humans when we are less than honest. We justify our lies as a necessary evil. The Bible tells us in Matthew 15:18 NIV, "But the things that come out of a person's mouth come from the heart, and these defile them."

See, we defile ourselves with our lies, as minuscule as they may be. Then we have trouble reconciling that there is a God who is perfect and holy, a God who cannot tell a lie. Numbers 23:19 NIV says it like this, "God is not human, that he should lie, not a human being, that he should change his mind. Does he speak and then not act? Does he promise and not fulfill?"

Unfortunately, we do not give God the credit due Him. Many times we look at God the same way we look at ourselves. We think that He may or may not do what He says because we have conditioned ourselves to believe God is as unreliable as a human.

Our God is a gracious God, a God who has made many promises to those who believe in Him. And if He has promised something, He cannot go back on that promise. Unfortunately, many people are not living in the promises of God because they do not know them.

Do you know what God has promised his children? If not, the pages of the Bible are filled with promises. Likewise, this devotional is scattered with the promises of God. Stick with it and learn what you are entitled to as a believer.

Verses to Ponder:

In hope of eternal life, which God, who does not lie, promised before the beginning of time. Titus 1:2 NIV

And also the glory of Israel will not lie or have regret, for he is not a man, that he should have regret. 1 Samuel 15:29 ESV

If we are faithless, he remains faithful- for he cannot deny himself. 2 Timothy 2:13 ESV

Sanctify them by the truth; your word is truth. John 17:17 NIV

Day 9

Who Is Your protector?

BEFORE READING | AFTER READING

Who is your protector? Why did you choose them?

Sometimes, protection means preserving our mental state. What do you need to let go of so you can protect your thoughts?

Before reading, I feel...

After reading, I feel...

What are three attributes of your protector?

Do you view God as a protector?

Has He protected you from anything in your life?

How has your perception of God changed after today's reading?

A Protector

On the journal page, I asked who your protector was and why. There is no doubt in my mind that the answers to this simple question will vary widely. Some may pick a spouse, a parent, a friend, or even themselves. Then there may be someone who has felt totally victimized by life and feels like they have never had a protector.

How we feel and how we look at life, as mentioned before, is determined by the experiences we have had. When I met my first husband, I was broken. As a young child, I had been molested by my cousins. Anytime I was at a family gathering, such as a funeral, I felt like a little girl again; I was scared, almost to the point of vomiting.

When my late-husband, Tim, a rough and tumble man who could take care of both him and me, was around, I felt safe. I felt as if no one in the world could hurt me. He was my protector. When he died, I lost that feeling of peace. Luckily for me, I had far removed myself from that side of the family.

That was until my uncle died. I loved my uncle, so I attended his funeral. There stood the men who had hurt me so long ago. I was terrified. No longer did I have my protector with me. I reverted back to a scared child, although I was in my late 30s. I was filled with hate; my heart pounded; I trembled with fear; my stomach rocked back and forth. All the while, I played out scenarios of how I would react if they talked to me.

Would I scream? Would I run? What would I do?

In the end, I had worked myself into an emotional wreck; it would take me weeks to calm down from that experience.

As I look back, I think I truly believed that without Tim, I was helpless. From the time I was 22, he had protected me. His hotheaded attitude was one to be reckoned with. All my victimizers would have had to do was look at us the wrong way, and Tim would have taken care of it. Now, I was forced to face the demons of my past without him. I will say it was an experience that I would learn from.

As weeks rolled into months and months into years, I was able to put the anxiety behind me. Then I got the call that my cousin, with whom I was very close, had died of cancer. Here we go again. I knew that these men would be at the funeral, and I would have to attend that funeral alone because of the virus that loomed.

As I fretted and worried, I realized that although I thought I had forgiven the wrong that was done to me, I realized my reaction to seeing them proved I had not. So, I began to pray.

The funny thing is, even being a seasoned Christian, I was holding on to the fear of this trauma, almost like a badge. I had not truly given it over to God. I had not truly asked Him to be my protector.

So, as I sat in my car, ice pouring through my veins, despite the heat pouring from the vents, I asked God to heal me, protect me, and deliver me from this awful experience. It was then my cousins pulled up. For the first time, as I looked at these men, I was no longer afraid, angry, or resentful. I just felt pity. I felt pity because I knew where my eternal home would be, pity because I had risen above the stress and drama of living my life for me. I had truly forgiven them for something for which they didn't ask me to forgive them.

The First 30 Days

That day I realized, although it was wonderful having Tim as my protector, there was someone I could depend on who would never leave, someone who could always protect me. That someone is God.

The Bible tells us in 2 Thessalonians 3:3 NIV, "But the Lord is faithful, and he will strengthen you and protect you from the evil one." Sometimes that protection does not mean we will not go through tough things. There are times when we will be strengthened to handle this world's pains and times when we will escape from them.

I wish I knew an exact formula to deter all pain from our lives, but that is not the case. I do know that Proverbs 2:11 NIV says, "Discretion will protect you, and understanding will guard you." Therefore, there are times when we put ourselves in situations that cause pain and then say, "God did not protect me," when, in fact, the situation could have turned out much worse.

See, God is the ultimate protector, but our free will and the free will of others also play a role in our lives. We will not always escape trials. Second Corinthians 4:8-9 NIV says, "We are hard-pressed on every side, but not crushed; perplexed, but not in despair; persecuted, but not abandoned; struck down, but not destroyed."

Although we will face trials, God will protect us from the enemy. We may have to walk through a valley, but when we are on the mountain top, that valley will seem so far away if we allow God to use for our good, what the devil meant for evil.

Verses to Ponder:

But let all who take refuge in you be glad; let them ever sing for joy. Spread your protection over them, that those who love your name may rejoice in you. Psalms 5:11 NIV

Though I walk in the midst of trouble, you preserve my life. You stretch out your hand against the anger of my foes; with your right hand you save me. Psalms 138:7 NIV

My God is my rock, in whom I take refuge, my shield and the horn of my salvation. He is my stronghold, my refuge and my savior— from violent people you save me. I called to the LORD, who is worthy of praise, and have been saved from my enemies. 2 Samuel 22:3-4 NIV

I give them eternal life, and they shall never perish; no one will snatch them out of my hand. My Father, who has given them to me, is greater than all; no one can snatch them out of my Father's hand. I and the Father are one. John 10:28-30 NIV

Day 10

What Are Your Needs?

Need-Meeter

Are your needs met? I'm not talking about your wants, I mean your needs. Do you have food, clothing, and shelter?

Often, we confuse our wants with our needs. I want a bigger vehicle. I do not need one. Although my car is cramped, it gets us around. We live in a country that has been blessed with such abundance that many of us do not even worry about where the basics are going to come from. We have running water, a stocked refrigerator, and a home to live in.

We forget that others are not as fortunate as us. We forget that our needs are really miniscule compared to all we have. When we forget this, we begin to mistake our wants for our needs. We begin to want more and more; we begin to believe we are entitled to what we want. This entitlement causes us to focus less on God and more on obtaining our wants.

We begin depending on ourselves, our abilities, our spouses, our families, or our government to meet what we perceive as our needs. We must step back from this line of thinking and realize what our needs really are. When we realize many of the things we think we need are purely wants, we begin to look at life and God a little differently.

God is the ultimate need-meeter, not want-meeter. The Bible tells us in Philippians 4:19 NIV, "And my God will meet all your needs according to the riches of his glory in Christ Jesus." Now, this verse does not say God will supply all your wants. Want a new car? Here it is. Want a hefty bank account? Done.

No, this verse says God will supply all your needs.

The First 30 Days

There is a big difference between a need and a want. In today's society we have blurred the lines between a need and a want. People want the biggest house, the nicest shoes, the best job; all the while they are leaving God out of the decision-making process to obtain their wants and not even trusting Him with their needs. When you exclude God from your decision-making or your life, you limit His ability to help you.

It is only when we rely on God that He can fully show His magnificence. Once we learn to trust in Him, not only does our focus begin to change from the things of this world to the things of God, but we also learn that God's provision means more than having the newest, nicest, trendiest thing. God's provision encompasses our whole being: mind, finances, relationships, physical needs, desires, and so much more.

The key to obtaining these things lies in our relationship with God. When we focus our mind on Him, He can also begin to bless us with our wants, because His wants become our wants.

Verses to Ponder:

But seek first his kingdom and his righteousness, and all these things will be given to you as well.
Matthew 6:33 NIV

The lions may grow weak and hungry, but those who seek the LORD lack no good thing. Psalms 34:10 NIV

If you remain in me and my words remain in you, ask whatever you wish, and it will be done for you. John 15:7 NIV

So do not fear, for I am with you; do not be dismayed, for I am your God. I will strengthen you and help you; I will uphold you with my righteous right hand.
Isaiah 41:10 NIV

Day 11

Who Are You in Relationship With?

BEFORE READING AFTER READING

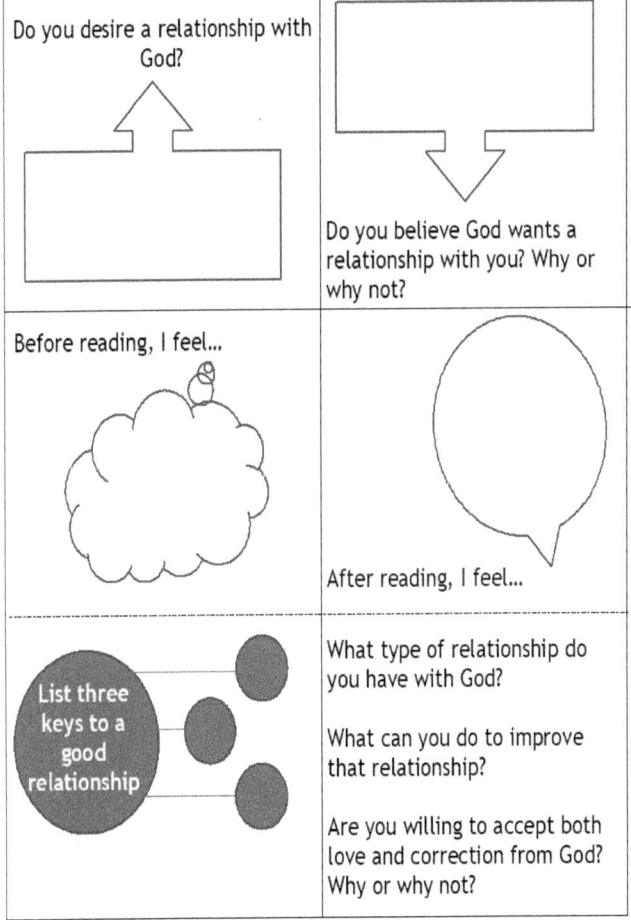

Do you desire a relationship with God?

Do you believe God wants a relationship with you? Why or why not?

Before reading, I feel...

After reading, I feel...

List three keys to a good relationship

What type of relationship do you have with God?

What can you do to improve that relationship?

Are you willing to accept both love and correction from God? Why or why not?

Relationship Seeker

God is more than a mythical man in the sky. He is a Father who desires a relationship with His children. Within that relationship, you will find that He will show His true character to you. Without a relationship with Him, you will lack in so many areas of your life.

Think of it this way: Let's say you have a loving father full of integrity who is willing to help you get your first good job. He has watched you work hard and become the best at what you do. He knows that you deserve to be in a better position; all you need are the right connections. So, he comes to you and tells you he will show your resume to a friend.

Now, if you had not been in a relationship with your father, he would never have known how hard you worked or how good you were at your job. He would not have recommended you based on your abilities because he would not have known them. Likewise, if you are out of a relationship with your father, it is harder to know what you need.

See, to be in a healthy relationship, you have to know the other person on more than a casual level. You have to spend time with them, learn about them, and respect them. This is all that God wants from His children. He wants to bless us, protect us, provide for us, and He will spend our whole life trying to come into relationship with us.

The Bible tells us in Ezekiel 34:11 AMPC, "For thus says the Lord God: 'Behold I, I Myself, will search for My sheep and will seek them out.'" We are His sheep. God created this earth so that He could enjoy it with the human race.

The First 30 Days

Adam and Eve were able to walk with God and talk with God until their sin separated them from Him. I find it interesting that in Genesis 3:8 NIV, Adam and Eve hid from God. He did not hide from them. All God wanted to do was spend time with them, but instead He had to search for them. Since that time, God has been forced to play the most important game of hide-and-seek known to man, a game with eternal consequences.

Unfortunately, even though God desires to be in relationship with each of us, He has given us free will. We must make a choice.

I love the parable of the wayward son in Luke 15:11-31 NIV. In this parable there is a son who has strayed from his father's house. While he was gone, the father had no idea where he was or what he needed. The boy, who had done everything wrong, realized his life would be better as a servant for his father than as a free man under someone with whom he had no relationship.

Despite the son's transgressions, when his father saw him coming home, he rejoiced and called for a feast. The father was so happy to be able to provide for his son that he forgot about the trouble he had caused and the money he squandered. The only thing that mattered to the father was that he had a chance to be in a relationship with his son once again.

God is like this father; He will welcome you back home if only you let Him. The choice is yours. God will never force you to love Him, but you cannot expect to be blessed by God without being His Child. To be blessed by God, you need to be in a true relationship with Him. You have to be willing not only to be blessed, but also to be rebuked. You have to be willing to grow and become closer to God. And with this growth, you must not just accept the blessing, but also the correction.

Verses to Ponder:

But the Lord God called to Adam and said to him, 'Where are you?' **Genesis 3:9 AMP**

You will seek me and find me when you seek me with all your heart. **Jeremiah 29:13 NIV**

For the Son of man came to seek and save the lost. Luke 19:10 NIV

The Lord is not slow to fulfill his promise as some count slowness, but is patient toward you, not wishing that any should perish, but that all should reach repentance. **2 Peter 3:9 ESV**

I will seek the lost, bring back the scattered, bind up the broken and strengthen the sick, but the fat and the strong I will destroy, I will feed them with judgment. Ezekiel 34:16 NASB

Day 12

Why Discipline?

BEFORE READING | **AFTER READING**

How were you disciplined as a child? How did this interaction affect the way you look at discipline?

After reading, did your idea of discipline change? If so, how?

Before reading, I feel...

After reading, I feel...

What are the three top traits of healthy discipline?

After reading, what had the most impact on you today?

What have you learned through your trials?

Discipline

I lived with my grandparents for a time in my life. I absolutely loved them. In the summer, I would stay at home with my grandpa during the day while my grandma was at work. We would watch TV, talk, play games, and I would cook for him, or we would sneak off to get a fish sandwich from a local restaurant.

When I was about eight, I remember being exceptionally hateful with my grandpa. I cannot remember what it was about, but I remember yelling at him.

Now, my grandpa was a big man who had served in the military. Unfortunately, many years of smoking and poor life choices had left him on oxygen and in poor health. Well, on this day, he wasn't feeling the best, so when I smarted-off, he whipped me with his oxygen hose.

If you have never been whipped with an oxygen hose, you have never been whipped. I would take my grandma's wooden spoon any day over that hose. It hurt, it left a welt, it was painful, but I never smarted-off to him again. I had learned my lesson.

The Bible tells us in Hebrews 12:11 ESV, "For the moment all discipline seems painful rather than pleasant, but later it yields the peaceful fruit of the righteousness to those who have been trained by it." See, I am positive I did not like it when I was disciplined. In fact, I hated it, but I learned the lesson not to disrespect my grandfather. In fact, I am so happy for the virtues he instilled in me before he died, virtues of respecting others, respecting our country, and respecting the men and women who fought for our rights.

There are times when we all need to be disciplined. If we were left to our own devices, we would not learn.

Think back to a person you have known, someone you know who was never told "no," a person who is selfish and self-centered. Many times, this person was never taught any better.

Just like our natural disciplinarians, God sometimes must discipline us. Now, that does not mean He will throw lightning bolts at your head. This isn't a Hollywood drama.

No, God is fair. Deuteronomy 8:5 ESV says, "Know then in your heart as a man disciplines his son, so the Lord your God disciplines you." Now, the way you look at this verse has a lot to do with the type of discipline you received growing up. If you had a father who went overboard, you might fear God. If you had a father who did not discipline you, you might not have reverence for God.

Regardless of the type of father you had, God is not bound by human emotions. He is fair. Second Chronicles 19:7 ESV says, "Now then, let the fear of the Lord be upon you. Be careful what you do, for there is no injustice with the Lord our God or partiality or taking bribes."

To please God, we need to be in relationship with Him. Once there, our hearts begin to turn from the things of this world to the things of God. The truth is, the closer you grow to God, the more refined you become.

See, we cannot look at God's discipline in the same way we look at a worldly view of discipline. That is because if we were to get what we deserve, we would all be going to hell. Instead, Jesus bore our sins on the cross. (1 Peter 2:24 NIV) If we are a born again believer, we no longer have to pay for our own sins with death. We will be able to love freely and live in eternity.

Yet we do not get what we deserve. No, our discipline comes on this side of the grave. Sometimes it comes in the form of consequences to our own actions. See, if God cleaned up all the messes we made in our lives, we would never learn to stop making those messes.

Other times, we endure trials and tribulations that are meant to enhance our faith and bring us closer to God the Father and His Son Jesus. James 1:2-4 NIV says, "Consider it pure joy, my brothers and sisters, whenever you face trials of many kinds because you know that the testing of your faith produces perseverance. Let perseverance finish its work so that you may be mature and complete, not lacking anything."

Now, do not take this into a ditch! I am NOT saying God causes these things. There is a very real devil that is hell-bent on destroying us. Although God could deliver us from all troubles the devil throws at us, what would we learn? Would we learn to trust in God? Or would we just become entitled little Christian brats who never grew in Christ?

God's discipline is so far out of our realm of understanding. While we see the world in our limited view, God knows the whole picture and He is working all things together for our good. (Romans 8:28 NIV)

Verses to Ponder:

Whoever spares the rod hates their children, but the one who loves their children is careful to discipline him. Proverbs 13:24 NIV

Whoever heeds discipline shows the way to life, but whoever ignores correction leads others astray.

Proverbs 10:17 NIV

*Those whom I love I rebuke and discipline.
So be earnest and repent.* Revelations 3:19 NIV

*A rod and a reprimand impart wisdom,
but a child left undisciplined disgraces its mother.
When the wicked thrive, so does sin,
but the righteous will see their downfall. Discipline
your children, and they will give
you peace; they will bring you the delights you desire.*
Proverbs 29:15-17 NIV

*Blessed is the one whom God corrects;
so do not despise the discipline of the Almighty. For
he wounds, but he also binds up;
he injures, but his hands also heal.* Job 5:17-18 NIV

*"And have you completely forgotten this word of
encouragement that addresses you as a father
addresses his son? It says, 'My son, do not make light of
the Lord's discipline, and do not lose heart when he
rebukes you, because the Lord disciplines the one he
loves, and he chastens everyone he accepts as his son.'
Endure hardship as discipline; God is treating you as
his children. For what children are not disciplined by
their father? If you are not disciplined—and everyone
undergoes discipline—then you are not legitimate, not
true sons and daughters at all. Moreover, we have all
had human fathers who disciplined us and we
respected them for it. How much more should we
submit to the Father of spirits and live!* Hebrews 12:5-9 NIV

Day 13

Who Is Your Role Model?

BEFORE READING

AFTER READING

Who is your role model?

Do you believe God is the ultimate role model? Why or why not?

Before reading, I feel...

After reading, I feel...

What are the first three attributes of your role model?

Do you allow God to be your role model?

Do you listen when the Holy Spirit speaks to you?

How can you improve your actions so they line up with the Word of God?

A Role Model

Most of us can think back on our lives and picture someone influential to us, someone we would turn to for advice when making tough decisions, someone we considered a good role model.

Although it is great to have someone in your corner who will lead and guide you, that person can sometimes steer you wrong. Let's face it, even a wise person can misread a situation or lack the ability to know what is truly in your heart. See, as humans, both our limited view of a situation and a person's willingness to share pertinent information play a role in the type of advice given.

So, even if you have a great person in your corner, one who gives wonderful advice, they may fail you at times. But there is someone who will never fail you, someone who knows the inner workings of your heart and soul, someone who can lead and guide you in a way no one else can. That Someone is the King of Kings and Lord of Lords, God.

See, God is the ultimate role model. Throughout His word, first through His actions and then through His son's actions, He shows us how to conduct ourselves. The Bible tells us, in Ecclesiastes 1:9, "What has been will be again, what has been done will be done again; there is nothing new under the sun." You see, nothing we go through will stump God. Within the pages of His Holy Word, He has already given us a solution.

Likewise, He has also given us the Holy Spirit to help guide us along our life path. John 14:26 says, "But the Advocate, the Holy Spirit, whom the Father will send in my name, will teach you all things and will remind you of everything I have said to you."

When you know Jesus as your personal Savior, as you read God's Word, it begins to speak to you. You begin to have revelations about your life and the situations you face. These revelations will come in the form of Bible verses, gut feelings, and yes, even by way of the Godly people in your life.

In all, God will use any means He chooses to help you live your best life. The Bible tells us in Hebrews 13:8 NIV, "Jesus Christ is the same yesterday and today and forever." He will not change to fit our world system. He is the only constant role model we will ever have.

It is up to you whether you live by His example or decide to live by the example of the world.

Verses to Ponder:

Whoever claims to live in him must live as Jesus did.
1 John 2:6 **NIV**

Follow my example, as I follow the example of Christ. 1 Corinthians 11:1 **NIV**

To this you were called, because Christ suffered for you, leaving you an example that you should follow in his steps. 1 Peter 2:21 **NIV**

Join together in following my example, brothers and sisters, and just as you have us as a model, keep your eyes on those who live as we do. Philippians 3:17 **NIV**

Dear friend, do not imitate what is evil but what is

good. Anyone who does what is good is from God. Anyone who does what is evil has not seen God. 3 John 1:11 **NIV**

Day 14

What is a Legacy?

BEFORE READING   **AFTER READING**

What does it mean to leave a legacy?

Which verse from today's reading stood out the most? Why?

Before reading, I feel...

After reading, I feel...

When you think of your life as a whole, what experiences have shaped how you view your life?

After reading, how has your idea of leaving a leagacy changed?

What legacy do you want to leave?

What steps will you take to leave your legacy?

The First 30 Days

Legacy-Leaver

I waited until I was older to have children, not because I did not want them but because, in my mind, if I waited, I would be able to provide a better life for them. See, I wanted my children to have the very best life possible. I wanted to be able to leave them with a legacy. Merriam-Webster defines legacy as "something transmitted by or received from an ancestor or predecessor from the past."

When I was thinking about children, my main focus was on the monetary aspects of a legacy. I did not want my children to have to take out ungodly amounts of student loans to go to college. I did not want my children to have to struggle. I wanted to be able to enjoy life with them and help them when appropriate.

As I have grown in Christ, I have realized there is more to leaving a legacy for your children than just providing for them. The most important legacy you can leave your children is a legacy of loving and serving God. See, most of the time, children grow up to imitate what they see. If they see a bad example, they tend to follow down that path. Likewise, the same is true for a good example. Leaving a legacy of following God can and will produce fruit in your child's life.

Just as I desire to leave a legacy for my children, God desires to leave a legacy for His children, a legacy of love, favor, power, and perseverance. The Bible says, "Know therefore that the Lord your God is God; he is the faithful God, keeping his covenant of love to a thousand generations of those who love him and keep his commandments." (Deuteronomy 7:9 NIV)

Can you imagine the implications of serving God for your family? This verse tells us God will keep His covenant to a thousand generations. As I was thinking about my legacy, I thought not only of my grandchildren and great-grandchildren, but a thousand generations. THAT IS A LEGACY!

See, God's plan for our lives is to prosper us; it says so in Jeremiah 29:11 NIV. That does not mean it will be easy, but God wants to leave a legacy for future generations. In order to do that, He has given us the tools we need to overcome the devil. God will make a way for us, even when there seems to be no way.

From the beginning of creation, He has desired to be in covenant with us, thereby leaving a legacy that can never be taken away.

Verses to Ponder:

I will establish my covenant as an everlasting covenant between me and you and your descendants after you for the generations to come, to be your God and the God of your descendants after you.
Genesis 17:7 NIV

The Lord said to Jehu, 'Because you have done well in accomplishing what is right in my eyes and have done to the house of Ahab all I had in mind to do, your descendants will sit on the throne of Israel to the fourth generation.' 2 Kings 10:30 NIV

We will not hide them from their descendants; we will tell the next generation the praiseworthy deeds of the

Lord, his power, and the wonders he has done. Psalms 78:4 **NIV**

A good person leaves an inheritance for their children's children, but a sinner's wealth is stored up for the righteous. Proverbs 13:22 **NIV**

Day 15

What Do You Choose?

BEFORE READING

AFTER READING

What choices do you find hard to make?

How do you feel that choosing to make God the Lord of your life will change your life?

Before reading, I feel...

After reading, I feel...

List three choices you are facing right now.

Have you heard the knock of God on the door of your heart?

If you have heard the knock, have you fully submitted to His authority?

How can God help you through this process?

You Choose

Every day we wake up, we have choices to make. Some can be as minor as what to wear for the day, or which song to listen to on the way to work. Others can have lasting impacts on our lives. Each decision, no matter how big or small it may be, is ours to make. We cannot depend on anyone else to make our decisions for us. In fact, we must take responsibility for our own actions or inactions.

Choosing to follow God/Jesus is no different. The Bible tells us in Revelation 3:20 NIV, "Here I am! I stand at the door and knock. If anyone hears my voice and opens the door, I will come in and eat with that person, and they with me." Being in God's presence brings an incomprehensible peace, but it does not negate the challenges of life.

In fact, choosing to follow Jesus is not always the easiest. There are times when you will not understand how things could happen. Then there are times you will be overjoyed with the way your life is going. The hills and valleys of life do not stop just because you decide to follow God; with His help, they just get easier to bear.

When we choose to live for something outside of ourselves, we begin to have a whole new perspective on life. As you read on, you will learn more about my walk with Jesus. Within my personal stories you will learn about God's place in my life and what He can do for you if you trust in Him.

Verses to Ponder:

For God so loved the world, that he gave his only son, that whoever believes in him shall not perish but have eternal life. John 3:16 NIV

But to all who did receive him, who believed in his name, he gave the right to become children of God. John 1:12 ESV

Because, if you confess with your mouth that Jesus is Lord and believe in your heart that God raised him from the dead, you will be saved. Romans 10:9 ESV

For the wages of sin is death, but the free gift of God is eternal life in Christ Jesus our Lord. Romans 6:23 NIV

For many are called, but few are chosen. Matthew 22:14 KJV

Day 16

Are You Deceived?

BEFORE READING **AFTER READING**

Deception

The devil is the author of deception. He has long twisted the words of people and God alike to suit his deeds. As the Bible tells us in John 8:44, the devil is the author of lies. So, it stands to reason, if he has been a liar from the beginning, he will not stop being a liar with you.

In fact, from the foundations of the world, the devil has been deceiving people. In the book of Genesis, God tells Adam "but you must not eat from the tree of the knowledge of good and evil..." (Genesis 2:17 NIV) Then, in Genesis 3 NIV, the devil entered. Through a play on words, he convinced Eve to eat from the tree of the knowledge of good and evil, causing a rift, a gap, between man and God.

See, the devil's main goal still is to cause a rift between you and God. Like with Eve, he will manipulate a situation to draw you into his web of lies. For me, his web of lies almost consumed me.

When my first husband passed away, it was a tragic night, filled with images it took years to overcome. Although I was a faithful church member, surrounded by wonderful people, I fell into a pit of despair. The doctor prescribed me alprazolam (alprazolam is prescribed for anxiety disorders and anxiety related to depression) and I began taking it immediately. I wasn't eating, couldn't sleep, and I was popping those pills.

See, I needed something to block out the pain that was engulfing me. I was being attacked from every side. Then I received a phone call that will forever be etched in my mind; someone I love and care for said horrible things to me. I know now that they were talking out of pain, but at the time, that was just the ammunition the

The First 30 Days

devil needed. It was the last straw, some might say. I began to spiral faster down the dark hole of despair and depression.

Now, the funny thing about me is, I was responsibly depressed. I still tried to make everything ok for everyone around me. I tried to take care of everyone else's feelings but my own. I couldn't think. I couldn't process what I had seen. I couldn't understand how I could be a widow with a baby. After all, my husband and I had prayed for him to be healed. I believed he would be healed. Then he died.

I began to believe the lies that the devil was feeding me, lies that God didn't care about me, lies that things would never get better, lies that my life had all been a lie. LIES! LIES! LIES. The more I believed the lies going through my mind, the farther and deeper I fell into despair.

Looking back, I now realize I had taken my eyes off Jesus and placed them on my situation. When we do this, it is the perfect opportunity for the devil to twist and manipulate any situation to his advantage. Our life gets darker and darker as we focus on our pain.

Unfortunately, just as easy as it was for the devil to manipulate Eve, someone who had walked and talked with God in the flesh, it is just as easy, if not easier, for the devil to manipulate us.

The Bible tells us in 2 Corinthians 11:3 ESV, "But I am afraid that just as the serpent's cunning deceived Eve, your minds may somehow be led astray from your sincere and pure devotion to Christ."

There are so many ways the devil will try to lead us astray. He may use the situations in our lives, the people, our own wants and desires, or merely our doubt and unbelief.

Either way, the devil's main objective is to take as many people as he can to the pit of hell with him; attacking our minds is his number one tactic.

Verses to Ponder:

Beloved, do not believe every spirit, but test the spirits to see whether they are from God, for many false prophets have gone out into the world. 1 John 4:1 ESV

See to it that no one takes you captive by philosophy and empty deceit, according to human tradition, according to the elemental spirits of the world, and not according to Christ. Colossians 2:8 ESV

I appeal to you, brothers, to watch out for those who cause divisions and create obstacles contrary to the doctrine that you have been taught; avoid them. For such persons do not serve our Lord Christ, but their own appetites,
and by smooth talk and flattery they deceive the hearts of the naïve. Romans 16:17-18 ESV

...while evil people and impostors will go on from bad to worse,
deceiving and being deceived. 2 Timothy 3:13 ESV

And the great dragon was thrown down, that ancient serpent, who is called the devil and Satan, the deceiver of the whole world—he was thrown down to the earth, and his angels were thrown down with him.
Revelation 12:9 ESV

Do not be deceived: God is not mocked, for whatever one sows, that will he also reap. For the one who sows to his own flesh will from the flesh reap corruption, but the one who sows to the Spirit will from the Spirit reap eternal life. And let us not grow weary of doing good, for in due season we will reap, if we do not give up.
Galatians 6:7-9 ESV

Day 17

What Are Your Hardships?

BEFORE READING

What hardships have you faced?

Before reading, I feel...

List three ways you deal with hardships in your life.

AFTER READING

Looking back, what did God use to help you through a situation that was plaguing you?

After reading, I feel...

What causes you to lose focus in a trial?

What can you do to improve your action or reaction in a trial?

When going through a trial, do you run from God or lean on Him?

Hardships & Help

Yesterday, I spoke of the lowest point in my life. During this time, I began to doubt all that I had known. As I said, I started a downward spiral that would throw me even deeper into the pit of despair. Although I was still going to church, I began to doubt what I knew was truth. As you read, I began to take alprazolam and slipped deeper into depression. I began to believe the lies that were racing in my head.

Then one afternoon, curtains drawn, baby sleeping, I began to have thoughts of suicide. I sat on my couch, running the events of the previous months through my mind. I felt betrayed not only on a worldly level, but also on a Godly level. My life had been riddled with pain and despair. I had had my fair share of trauma, and now this too! How could I go on? I was broken, I was hurting, and I just wanted the pain to end.

I stood up and began pacing back and forth; I honestly had decided I was done with all the pain. It was at that moment that my phone rang. My boss at the time said she had a weird feeling and felt like she needed to call and check on me. Shortly after we talked, I heard my little man begin to cry.

It was like a light went off. What was I thinking? I had a baby that had just lost his father, and I was so selfish as to want to end my own pain. That was a turning point for me.

See, there are times in your life when God will use other people to reach you. He will send you a life preserver to pull you from the pit of hell that you are in.

Not one of us will escape this life without trials. We

will all face hard times. Some of us, it seems, will endure more hard times than others, but we all will endure trials of one kind or another. The Bible tells us, "I have told you these things, so that in me you may have peace. In this world, you will have trouble. But take heart! I have overcome the world." (John 16:33 NIV)

When we are in the middle of the trial, it is easy for us to lose focus. Pain changes the way we think. It can cloud our minds and make us take our focus off the things of God. But the Bible tells us, "God is our refuge and strength, an ever-present help in trouble." (Psalm 46:1 NIV)

If we focus on God and not on our circumstances, He will help us through. There is no limit to what God will do to reach His children. He will use the Bible, the Holy Spirit, a still, small voice, and other people to comfort, give peace, and bring guidance.

But just as I mentioned earlier, you have a choice if you want to accept the help given. Our God is a gentleman. He will never force help upon you, even when it is for your own good.

Verses to Ponder:

Count it all joy, my brothers, when you meet trials of various kinds, for you know that the testing of your faith produces steadfastness. And let steadfastness have its full effect, that you may be perfect and complete, lacking in nothing. James 1:2-4 ESV

Not only that, but we rejoice in our sufferings, knowing that suffering produces endurance, and endurance

produces character, and character produces hope, and hope does not put us to shame, because God's love has been poured into our hearts through the Holy Spirit who has been given to us. Romans 5:3-5 ESV

Blessed is the man who remains steadfast under trial, for when he has stood the test he will receive the crown of life, which God has promised to those who love him. James 1:12 ESV

Day 18

Do You Doubt?

BEFORE READING	AFTER READING
Do you have doubts about God? If so, what are they?	How does it make you feel to know that someone so committed to God has been full of doubt and unbelief?
Before reading, I feel...	After reading, I feel...
List 1-3 things you doubt God can do.	Have you ever been fearful to share your feelings because of what others may think? If so, how did it affect your relationship with God? Have you prayed about the doubts you have? After reading Mark 9, what thoughts do you have?

The First 30 Days

Doubt & Unbelief

I would do you no favors during this time if I were not honest with you. As Christians, it is sometimes hard to admit that we have had periods of doubt and unbelief. After all, we have to keep up our appearances. We don't want to lose our status in the church. So instead of seeking guidance, we bottle up our thoughts and feelings.

I often wonder if this is part of the reason some people leave the faith. I once heard an old adage that said, "The bigger they are, the harder they fall." I believe this is true for our prayers also. If we believe something with all our heart and soul, and it doesn't come to pass, there are times it can rock our faith. Trust me, I know.

When my first husband received the diagnosis of cancer, I kicked into high gear. We prayed and listened to healing CDs; we went to the elders of the church. We did it all. I would not even talk to him about the possibility of him dying because I KNEW he was going to be healed.

So, on the night he went to his eternal home, I was crushed. After life settled in, and everyone went home, I was picking up the pieces of my life. I began to doubt God.

How could God do this to me? Does He even hear my prayers? Is He even real? On and on, my mind spiraled. I was devastated. I was angry. I wanted answers. I was at the lowest valley of my life, and I felt so alone at times. One moment I would feel as if God was surrounding me with His loving arms, and the next, I would doubt Him.

To top it all off, I felt guilty for having moments of doubt and unbelief. I was afraid to talk to anyone about my feelings because I already felt like people were judging how I was handling my life, my son, and my grief. So, I bottled it up. There were days when it took all I had to not yell and scream at God.

Luckily for me, God is a forgiving God. He understands our grief. He will stick with us through it all. The Bible tells us in Psalm 34:18 NLT, "The Lord is close to the brokenhearted; he rescues those whose spirits are crushed."

Looking back, I am sure I could have handled my grief better, but when you are in the throes of pain, you are blinded by your own circumstances.

As I sit here today, writing about my doubt and unbelief, I know that God will use for His own glory, what the devil intends for evil. If I would have had someone to set me down and tell me they also had felt doubt, maybe I would have worked through it much faster than I did.

So, even if you doubt in your heart, know that you can work through it. Even Thomas, one of Jesus' disciples, a man who walked with, learned from, and loved Jesus, had doubts. John 20:25 NIV says, "So the other disciples told him, 'We have seen the Lord!' But he said to them, 'Unless I see the nail marks in his hands and put my finger where the nails were, and put my hand into his side, I will not believe.'"

Although Thomas knew the teachings, he still doubted, but being a gracious God, in verse 27 NIV, Jesus appeared to Thomas and said, "Put your finger here; see my hands. Reach out your hand and put it into my side. Stop doubting and believe."

The First 30 Days

As Christians, there may be times in our lives when we have doubts. If one of Jesus' closest companions doubted, we too could go through a phase of doubt and unbelief. This is nothing to be ashamed about. We must work through our feelings. We must get into the Word of God. We must be like the father in Mark 9.

See, he went to Jesus to heal his son. When approaching Jesus, the father said in Mark 9:22 NIV, "...But, if you can do anything, take pity on us and help us." I love the interaction that takes place in the next two verses. Let's read them.

Mark 9:23-24 NIV: "If you can'?" said Jesus. "Everything is possible for one who believes. Immediately the boy's father exclaimed, 'I do believe; help me overcome my unbelief!'" Did you catch that? This man admitted his unbelief and then asked Jesus to help him overcome it, and his son was healed.

See, having doubts is something that will happen from time to time. The key is to be like this man and not allow your doubts to fester and pull you from the faith. As I look back, I thank God that He pulled me from my pit of doubt and unbelief. I am in such a better place in my life than I would have been without God.

So, the next time you have doubt creeping into your mind, go back to Mark 9 and remember that you are not alone.

But, most of all, remember that God can deliver you from your doubt just as He did for me, if only you allow Him to help.

Verses to Ponder:

So then faith come by hearing, and hearing by the word of God. Romans 10:17 NKJV

The thief comes only to steal and kill and destroy. I came that they may have life and have it abundantly. John 10:10 ESV

And if they do not persist in unbelief, they will be grafted in, for God is able to graft them in again. Romans 11:23 NIV

Even though I was once a blasphemer and a persecutor and a violent man, I was shown mercy because I acted in ignorance and unbelief. 1 Timothy 1:13 NIV

Day 19

What Is Power?

BEFORE READING | **AFTER READING**

Do you think there is power in a promise?

After reading, how would you define God's power?

Before reading, I feel...

After reading, I feel...

List three traits of a powerful person.

How can living in the fullness of God's love enhance your power in Him?

What comes to mind when you read, "There is a difference between someone who believes and lives as the world does, and someone who believes and walks in God's promises?"

Promises & Power

Psalm 30:5 NLT says, "For his anger lasts only a moment, but his favor lasts a lifetime! Weeping may last through the night, but joy comes with the morning."

Doubt and unbelief, weeping and pain, are emotions we are bound to feel in our lifetime, but these feelings only last for a moment if we trust Him. When we trust in the Lord, we gain power, power over disease, power over our circumstances, power over our thoughts. This power comes in the form of promises. Throughout the Word of God, we are given these promises to stand on, promises of peace, joy, redemption, reconciliation, and so many more.

To obtain these promises, you not only have to be part of the family, but you also have to know what you are entitled to as a child of God. See, we all have a choice to accept or reject God as our Father. The decision is ours, but I will tell you choosing God will help you through. I liken this choice to the choice I had when my mom met my stepdad.

My biological father killed himself when I was little. It was a very turbulent time for our family. My mom was young with two small children and was now a widow. Needless to say, times were tough.

My mom then met my stepdad, a hardworking, honest man who took in two girls who did not belong to him. Through the years, he has become our father; he is the only father my sister remembers. He is the father we can call if we have a problem. He is the father who jumped into action after my first husband died.

See, when my stepdad took us in, we not only gained a

father, but we also gained someone who would look out for us. If I had rejected him, I would not live in the fullness of his love, nor would I have the benefits of being his daughter. No, if I would have rejected him, I would have missed out on all the love, help, and wisdom he has given to me over the years.

Choosing to accept my father's gift of love and protection has made my life easier. Unfortunately, many do not have a father they can depend on. But there is a Heavenly Father who wants to love, protect, and bless you with His power. It is God the Father, and He has many promises you can walk in, if only you choose to do so.

In the next section, we will discuss the promises God has made to those who believe and follow Him. Truthfully, there is a difference between someone who believes and lives as the world does, and someone who believes and walks in God's promises.

Verses to Ponder:

I have given them Your word; and the world has hated them because they are not of the world, just as I am not of the world. I do not pray that You should take them out of the world, but that You should keep them from the evil one. They are not of the world, just as I am not of the world. John 17:14-16 NKJV

You adulterous people, don't you know that friendship with the world means enmity against God? Therefore, anyone who chooses to be a friend of the world becomes an enemy of God. James 4:4 NIV
Do not love this world nor the things it offers you, for

when you love the world, you do not have the love of the Father in you. For the world offers only a craving for physical pleasure, a craving for everything we see, and pride in our achievements and possessions. These are not from the Father, but are from this world. And this world is fading away, along with everything that people crave. But anyone who does what pleases God will live forever. 1 John 2:15-17 NLT

He predestined us for adoption to sonship through Jesus Christ, in accordance with his pleasure and will— to the praise of his glorious grace, which he has freely given us in the One he loves.
Ephesians 1:5-6 NIV

Day 20

Where Do You Get Your Power?

The First 30 Days

Power

There is power in the name of Jesus. The Bible tells us in Philippians 2:9-11 NIV, "Therefore God exalted him to the highest place and gave him the name that is above every name, that at the name of Jesus every knee should bow, in heaven and on earth and under the earth, and every tongue acknowledge that Jesus Christ is Lord, to the glory of God the Father."

The name above all other names. Have you ever thought about what that statement truly means, that the name of Jesus is above all else? It is above poverty, sickness, hate, depression, trials, and tribulations. IT IS ABOVE ALL!

If this is true, why aren't more people living successful lives?

Well, look at it this way. Many things in this world possess power of one type or another. Oxygen has the power to keep us alive, heal certain illnesses, and hasten chemical reactions. Most of the time, we take for granted the power that oxygen possesses.

Likewise, gasoline is a powerful substance. It has the power to increase a flame, destroy an object, and create energy. These two substances alone are powerful, but when combined in the carburetor of a vehicle, they become a force to be reckoned with. That said, have you ever thought about the process that goes into creating energy in a carburetor?

For your car to run properly, your carburetor must mix proper amounts of both air and gasoline. The mixture is then sent to the cylinders, where it produces a combustion with the help of sparkplugs. If you have too much oxygen or too much gasoline, your car will not run properly.

Although gasoline and oxygen both contain power, they must be appropriately mixed to produce the energy they need to run a car. If you fail to fill up your gas tank, your vehicle will not have power.

Our power in Jesus is just like the power required to run an engine. We must first have a relationship with Him. Knowing that He exists does not give you power. Just like knowing where the gas station is does not make your car run.

When we know Him as our Lord, we may then begin mixing our faith in such a way that we can see results.

Verses to Ponder:

But he said to me, 'My grace is sufficient for you, for my power is made perfect in weakness.' Therefore I will boast all the more gladly about my weaknesses, so that Christ's power may rest on me. 2 Corinthians 12:9 NIV

The message of the cross is foolish to those who are headed for destruction! But we who are being saved know it is the very power of God.
1 Corinthians 1:18 NLT

And through your faith, God is protecting you by his power until you receive this salvation, which is ready to be revealed on the last day for all to see.
1 Peter 1:5 NLT

Day 21

What Is Faith?

BEFORE READING   **AFTER READING**

How do you define faith?

How do you rate your faith on a scale between 1-10? Why?

Before reading, I feel...

After reading, I feel...

List three areas where you need more faith.

Do you believe faith is an action that produces a reaction? Why or why not?

Do you stand on the promises of God?

What does the story of Moses' mother speak to you?

The First 30 Days

Faith

Yesterday, I talked about the way an engine produces energy to run a vehicle. I likened the process of combustion to the power that is in the name of Jesus. Just as an engine cannot run without gasoline or air, our belief in God cannot run without faith. See, faith is an action, and just like any action, it causes a reaction.

Our faith action causes a faith reaction. The Bible tells us, "And without faith it is impossible to please God, because anyone who comes to him must believe that he exists and that he rewards those who earnestly seek him." (Hebrews 11:6 NIV) See, when we have faith, God will reward us in due time. Without faith, we are not pleasing to God.

Likewise, faith is knowing that you can trust God with anything. As a mother, I believe one of the greatest stories of faith is found in the Old Testament in Exodus 2. The story is about a baby named Moses. At the time, the Israelites were enslaved in Egypt. During their enslavement, Pharaoh saw the Israelites were multiplying, so he ordered the murder of all baby boys.

As a mother of sons, my heart breaks at this passage. I can almost feel the fear Moses' mother must have felt during her pregnancy. I imagine she had been praying for months for the child she felt growing in her womb. I could see her praying for a girl, praying for protection, just praying. Then, can you imagine the enormous burden she must have felt when her son Moses was born, and she realized there was a death sentence upon him?

Exodus 2:2-3 NIV tells us she hid Moses for three months, and when she could not hide him any longer,

The First 30 Days

she made a basket out of papyrus and placed him in the basket to float in the Nile.

Can you imagine the amount of preparation and prayer that would have gone into her decision to place her baby in the Nile? She had to have faith that her God would spare this baby she loved so. I can only imagine the agony in which she prayed as she let go and allowed God to protect Moses. See, she had to have faith that God would protect him because she could no longer do so.

The Bible tells us, "Now faith is the confidence in what we hope for and the assurance about what we do not see." (Hebrews 11:1 NIV) Put plainly, faith is knowing that although we do not see what we would like to see right now, we know God will see us through all situations. Faith is knowing that we have the promises of God to stand on. Faith is knowing that His word is living, powerful, true, and cannot be made void, despite what we are experiencing or thinking. Faith is taking our focus off us and placing it on Him. Faith is being like Moses' mother; when you reach the end of what you can accomplish on your own as she did, you trust God can do the rest.

Verses to Ponder:

Therefore I tell you, whatever you ask for in prayer, believe that you have received it,
and it will be yours. Mark 11:24 NIV

For we live by faith, not by sight. 2 Corinthians 5:7 NIV

Though you have not seen him, you love him; and even

though you do not see him now, you believe in him and are filled with an inexpressible and glorious joy, for you are receiving the end result of your faith, the salvation of your souls. 1 Peter 1:8-9 NIV

Accept the one whose faith is weak, without quarreling over disputable matters. Romans 14:1 NIV

Day 22

Is Your Faith Hindered?

Hindered Faith

Sitting here writing, I began to wonder why it was so hard to have faith in God. After all, we have faith every day in the things of this world. We have faith that our car will start, we will get paid for time worked, our heat will come on, and we even have faith in imperfect humans. Why is it so hard to have faith in a God who is perfect and whole?

Is it because we cannot comprehend His perfection? Or something deeper? The dictionary defines faith as "complete trust or confidence in someone or something." The truth is, to have complete faith in God, we have to depend less on the things of this world and more on the things of God.

Complete trust in God can be hard to accomplish. Each person has their own set of dependencies on relationships, careers, drugs, sex, gossip, etc. To fully depend on God, we have to let go of our dependencies and give them over to God. Even when our dependencies are destructive, it can be hard to give them up. They become a crutch to us, a known normal that becomes harder to let go of as time continues.

For the rich young ruler in Matthew 19:16-30, his crutch was his wealth. He was a good person who followed all of God's commands, but he depended more on his money than he did on God's ability to provide for him. In the end, his inability to let go of the things of this world and trust God hindered his faith.

We can be like this, too. Our faith is lacking for various reasons. In many cases, our faith is rooted in ourselves or in the things of this world. We tend to overlook God's abilities until we have reached the end of ourselves, when the situation is so bad we cannot handle it alone. This is not a sincere faith. Sincere faith depends on God first, not last. Thus, it will hinder our ability to see God in action.

Somewhere I read, "Faith is blind." I'm not sure that is true. To me, it seems, faith is looking head-on into the throes of adversity, seeing the obstacles laid out before you, and knowing that your God is bigger than anything this world can throw at you.

To me, the key to walking successfully in faith is activating it.

Verses to Ponder:

You ask and do not receive, because you ask wrongly, to spend it on your passions. James 4:3 ESV

But your iniquities have made a separation between you and your God, and your sins have hidden his face from you so that he does not hear. Isaiah 59:2 ESV

*The lord is not slow to fulfill his promise as some count slowness, but is patient towards you,
not wishing that any should perish, but that all should reach repentance.* 2 Peter 3:9 ESV

Do not be deceived: God is not mocked, for whatever one sows, that will he also reap. Galatians 6:7 ESV

Day 23

How Do You Activate Faith?

Activating Faith

The Bible tells us in Matthew 6:33 NIV, "But seek first his kingdom and his righteousness, and all these things will be given to you as well." To activate our faith, we must be connected to God; it must be a real spiritual connection, praying, seeking, reading, fasting, listening to, accepting correction from, and following His commands.

We cannot activate our faith by mere lip service to God. Unlike people, we cannot fool God. The Bible tells us that God knows our innermost thoughts. (Psalm 94:11) We must approach His throne of grace with humility and reverence while examining our own hearts.

I can remember when I was young in the faith that I would talk to God. I would say things like, "Well, I would start my own school if You would bless me with the money to do it." Now, this sounds like a spiritual request. After all, I wanted to start a Christian school where students could be challenged and stretched, one where they would learn about God and not have to deal with ungodly people.

The only problem was, my request was coming from the heart of aggravation. I was mad because my position had been cut. No longer would our school truly serve the High Ability kids. No longer would they be challenged and stretched. So, I spiritualized my aggravation and all but begged God to show me how to make a difference.

I was not seeking God first and then allowing my thoughts to line up with His. No, I was seeking me first and asking God to line up with me.

Looking back, I can see why God did not honor my request. First, as a young Christian, I would have messed it up. Secondly, I was not tapping into my faith, I simply wanted to get out of the trial.

To activate our faith and see results, we must align our thoughts with God's desires for our lives. The Bible tells us in Proverbs 16:1-3 ESV, "The plans of the heart belong to man, but the answer of the tongue is from the Lord. All the ways of a man are pure in his own eyes, but the Lord weighs the spirit. Commit your work to the Lord, and your plans will be established." When we commit our work to the Lord, our thoughts begin to line up with His.

Now, does this mean you will always get what you want when you want it? No! Sometimes we have to wait to see our faith produce the results we want to see.

Verses to Ponder:

I have been crucified with Christ. It is no longer I who live, but Christ who lives in me. And the life I now live in the flesh I live by faith in the Son of God, who loved me and gave himself for me.
Galatians 2:20 ESV

Therefore I tell you, whatever you ask for in prayer, believe that you have received it, and it will be yours. Mark 11:24 NIV

Look to the LORD and his strength; seek his face always.
Psalm 105:4 NIV

*'Even now,' declares the L*ORD*, 'return to me with all your heart, with fasting and weeping and mourning.'*
Joel 2:12 NIV

Day 24

Who Are You Waiting For?

BEFORE READING

Are you a patient person?

Before reading, I feel...

What are 1-3 things you have a hard time waiting for?

AFTER READING

Do you find waiting easier or harder when you are waiting on God to move? Explain.

After reading, I feel...

What have you learned from waiting on your answer?

How does your attitude impact the waiting process?

Is there anything you need to do to improve your attitude?

Waiting Faith

Waiting on the Lord is much like baking the Thanksgiving turkey. It takes hours to bake. First, you have to prep the turkey, then set it to roast for hours. Next, you have to crisp the skin, then finally, you can eat. It is not a short process.

Waiting on the Lord is much like that. You first have to activate your faith. Then you have to walk out your faith for what seems like forever. Next, you have to prepare for your miracle. Then finally, you can enjoy the fruits of your faith.

The Bible tells us, "Rejoice in hope, be patient in tribulation, be constant in prayer." (Romans 12:12 ESV) Sometimes, waiting on the Lord can be the biggest tester of faith, especially if you have nonbelievers criticizing you for your faith. Much like waiting on Thanksgiving dinner, the wait is worth the reward.

I remember when my first husband and I got married. I wanted a baby so badly. I wanted to be a mom, but I wanted to finish my degree first. The first time I got pregnant, I was over the moon. I could not have been happier. Then I had a miscarriage.

For years I prayed for another baby. My heart was broken. I was angry at all the people who had babies they did not take care of. I was angry at my body for not being able to conceive. I was just angry; I was still waiting for something I wanted more than anything else. Then one day, I gave it to God. I repented for my bad attitude, and I asked for a baby.

See, I had been bitter and angry all the time I had been waiting for my miracle. I wasn't ready to raise a child. As I waited, I fell more in love with this little human I had not even been given yet.

Finally, after many years of praying and soul searching, I became pregnant and gave birth to a wonderful baby boy, and all the time spent waiting was but like a moment.

Waiting on God is just as sweet when you have faith. I am by no means saying all of the time spent waiting is fun. Not at all. Sometimes, the waiting is torturous, but during that time you learn things about both yourself and God that will make you a better person.

So, when it doesn't seem as if God is working in your life, remember that sometimes we have to wait, because just like a Thanksgiving turkey or my beautiful baby boy, the wait is worth the reward.

Verses to Ponder:

But they who wait for the Lord shall renew their strength; they shall mount up with wings of eagles; they shall run and not grow weary; they shall walk and not faint. Isaiah 40:31   ESV

But if we hope for what we do not see, we wait for it with patience. Romans 8:25 ESV

Wait for the Lord, be strong and take heart and wait for the Lord. Psalm 27:14 NIV

But do not forget this one thing, dear friends: With the Lord a day is like a thousand years, and a thousand years are like a day. 2 Peter 3:8 NIV

Day 25

How Do You Increase Faith?

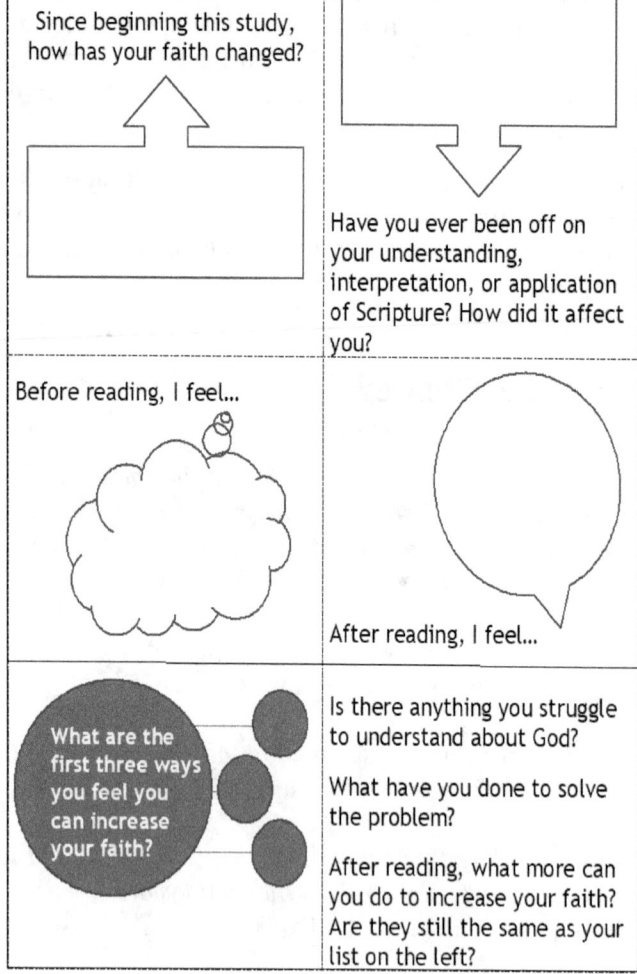

Increasing Faith

Faith is like a muscle. A muscle must be stretched and worked for it to grow. Likewise, if you gain muscle and then you sit on your couch day in and day out and never do anything, your muscles are eventually going to grow weak. Faith is the same way. To grow our faith, we must work at creating a strong faith base. Then we must continue to work our faith so that it grows strong and does not atrophy.

First, let's tackle growing our faith. The Bible tells us in Romans 10:17 ESV, "So faith comes from hearing, and hearing through the word of Christ." It is hard to have faith in something you do not know. In order to increase your faith, you must be in the Word of God. You must attend church. You must read your Bible. You must pray. These are all ways that we Christians learn what the Word of God says, how to interpret it, and how to apply it.

See, if we are off in any of these areas, understanding, interpretation, or application, we run the risk of doing more harm than good, not only with our own faith, but with the faith of others. In 2 Timothy 2:15 NKJV, the Bible tells us to rightly divide the word of truth. We must ensure that we are not just hearers of the Word, but also people who study, understand, and do the Word.

The Bible is like the greatest recipe ever written. It has all the ingredients, instructions, and examples you need to create a wonderful life, but you have to know what the ingredients are in order to use them properly.

With faith, the first ingredient is the Word of God. The Bible tells us in James 1:22 NIV, "Do not merely listen to the word, and so deceive yourselves, Do what it says." To do what we need to do, in order to increase our faith, we must know what we must do.

So, to increase our faith, we must be willing to dive into the Word of God and commit to doing what He has commanded us to do.

Verses to Ponder:

Your word is a lamp for my feet, a light on my path.
Psalm 119:105 NIV

For the word of God is alive and active. Sharper than any double-edged sword, it penetrates even to dividing soul and spirit, joints and marrow; it judges the thoughts and attitudes of the heart.
Hebrews 4:12 NIV

All Scripture is God-breathed and is useful for teaching, rebuking, correcting and training in righteousness, so that the servant of God may be thoroughly equipped for every good work. 2 Timothy 3:16-17 NIV

He replied, 'Blessed rather are those who hear the word of God and obey it.' Luke 11:28 NIV

Day 26

Do You Exercise Your Faith?

BEFORE READING | **AFTER READING**

Do you exercise your faith?

How do you face your trials with faith?

Before reading, I feel...

After reading, I feel...

List 1-3 times you had to exercise your faith?

How does exercising your faith help you to grown in christ?

Has God ever used an exercise in faith to help you learn more about Him? Explain.

Exercising Your Faith.

To grow your faith, you must be an active participant in exercising your faith muscle. I do not need faith to know that trials will come in my life. I do, on the other hand, need faith to face those trials.

A few years back, I was really sick. It seemed that one thing after another was attacking my body. After nursing my son, I had mastitis twice. I was so ill, I could not do anything but sleep. Once that trial was over, I moved on to the next.

One night, I woke up in severe pain. I was vomiting uncontrollably, and I felt as if my body were being ripped open from the inside out. No pain I had ever felt compared to the pain I was in.

At the ER, I was told I had pancreatitis. For months I dealt with the pain and sickness that came along with acute reoccurring pancreatitis. I had tests run, went to specialists, had an endoscopy done, but no one could determine what was causing the illness.

During this time, I prayed, I blogged, and I believed that I would be healed. As much as I would like to say my healing was instantaneous the moment I first prayed, it was not. I had to endure months of pain, doctors' appointments, procedures, and conflicting feelings. I had to fight to keep my faith strong, because the devil tried his best to keep me from receiving from God what He intended to give me: healing.

Now, to understand how amazing our God is, you have to understand how I approached this situation. I prayed. I talked to God. I had faith that I would be healed. In fact, when everyone else was concerned, I knew I was going to be healed. I didn't know when or

The First 30 Days

how, but I knew God would heal me.

So, I did not want to bother my pastor. I did not want to be that needy churchgoer bothering the pastor when there were so many other people who needed his time and attention.

Then one night at church, the pastor got up and said something to the effect that God had told him someone was dealing with pancreatic issues, and they are healed in Jesus' name.

Now, if I had gone to my pastor, this would not have been so amazing, but I had never gone to him. I had never missed church or told him I was even going through procedures. I had not given him any reason for him to have a word from God that affirmed my faith in healing. This was a faith I had struggled with since the death of my first husband.

The most amazing part of this story happened as my pastor spoke. As he spoke, it felt like a lightning bolt hit my head. Tingling radiated down my face, out to my arms, and through my midsection before finally exiting through my feet. In an instant, I knew I was healed.

Now, the Bible tells us to walk in wisdom, so I completed all the necessary tests I had scheduled. All tests showed I was truly healed.

See, sometimes, faith is not getting what you want at the time you want it. Sometimes, faith is genuinely about exercising your faith muscles. It is sticking to what you know God has promised to give you, even when you do not yet see the results of that promise.

Verses to Ponder:

But you, dear friends, by building yourselves up in your most holy faith and praying in the Holy Spirit, keep yourselves in God's love as you wait for the mercy of our Lord Jesus Christ to bring you to eternal life.
Jude 1:20-21 NIV

But when you ask, you must believe and not doubt, because the one who doubts is like a wave of the sea, blown and tossed by the wind. James 1:6 NIV

Be on your guard; stand firm in the faith; be courageous; be strong. 1 Corinthians 16:13 NIV

His master replied, 'Well done, good and faithful servant! You have been faithful with a few things; I will put you in charge of many things. Come and share your master's happiness!' Matthew 25:21 NIV

Day 27

What Are You Promised?

BEFORE READING | **AFTER READING**

Do know what you are promised?

After reading today, what patterns would you like to work on to improve your life?

Before reading, I feel...

After reading, I feel...

What are 1-3 problems you have that you need help with?

What verses can you stand on, in faith, to cover the problems you mentioned on the left?

How can God help you through this process?

Promises of God

The Bible is scattered with promises from God, promises we can stand on when times get tough. As I was doing research for this book, I learned of a man named Everett R. Storms who, on his 27th reading of the Bible, decided to count the promises contained therein. After reading the Bible in its entirety, he concluded God made 7,487 promises to man. (Knowles,1998)

The magnitude of a promise can be lost on us today, due to the unreliability of people. In today's society, our "yes" only means yes if it benefits us, or we have nothing better to do. Unfortunately, one's word is not a binding contract anymore.

Unlike humans, God does not take a promise lightly. When God makes a promise, it is settled. God is not human that He can lie. (Numbers 23:19 NIV) Therefore, when He makes a promise in His Word, it is as good as done, if we hold up our end of the bargain.

For the next few days, we will focus on a few all-encompassing promises found in the word of God. But first, you need to understand, the promises of God are **Yes** and **Amen**! Second Corinthians 1:20 NIV says, "For no matter how many promises God has made, they are "Yes" in Christ. And so through him the "Amen" is spoken by us to the glory of God."

God sent His only Son to die for us so that we may live in the shadow of the Almighty, if only we accept Him. (Psalm 91:1 NIV) Inside that shadow resides **peace** and a **hope** that surpass any circumstance you will face on this side of eternity. Romans 15:13 NIV says, "May the God of hope fill you with all joy and peace as you trust in him, so that you may overflow with hope by the power of the Holy Spirit."

Within this one verse we have a promise of joy, peace, hope, and power in the Holy Spirit. Four promises are wrapped into one verse. See, when we immerse ourselves in the Word of the Lord, we realize, with the help of Our Lord, there is nothing that we cannot tackle.

Speaking of tackling an issue, when my first husband died, I had horrible nightmares. The horrific scene laid in front of me was one that would have taken center stage in any horror movie. In my nightmares, it did just that. The scene played out over and over, night after night. It wasn't until I gave in and stopped trying to heal without God's help that I realized there was a peace and a hope in the loving arms of the Holy Spirit.

Over the years, the more I have learned to rely on God, the more peace I have made with the things I saw the night my first husband died. I was able to live inside the hope of knowing I will see him again one day in Heaven.

Seeing the world through the lens of faith changes your whole outlook on the situation. I am not saying that we will not endure trials or tribulations; I am saying, if we lean on Him, we will find peace.

Like I said earlier, God is not a man that He can lie. If He promises us peace, we will have peace. It may not be right at the moment we experience the challenge, but peace will come, just like all the promises of the Lord will come to fruition if we have faith and abide in Him.

Verses to Ponder:

For God so loved the world, that he gave his only son, that whoever believes in him should not perish but have eternal life. John 3:16 NIV

...but whoever listens to me will live in safety and be at ease, without fear of harm. Proverbs 1:33 NIV

But I tell you the truth, it is to your advantage that I go away; for if I do not go away, the Helper (Comforter, Advocate, Intercessor—Counselor, Strengthener, Standby) will not come to you; but if I go, I will send Him (the Holy Spirit) to you [to be in close fellowship with you.] John 16:7 AMP

'For I know the plans I have for you,' declares the LORD, 'plans to prosper you and not to harm you, plans to give you hope and a future.' Jeremiah 29:11 NIV

But the Lord is faithful, and He will strengthen you [setting you on a firm foundation] and will protect and guard you from the evil one. 2 Thessalonians 3:3 AMP

but those who hope in the LORD will renew their strength. They will soar on wings like eagles; they will run and not grow weary, they will walk and not be faint. Isaiah 40:31 NIV

Day 28

How Do You View Faith?

Freedom Promises

Many people look at the Word of God and see it as restrictive or stuffy: Do this. Don't do that. In the Bible, God has put forth a standard of living by which He desires us to live; these rules are there to enhance our lives, not hinder them.

In fact, the Word of God is not there to make life harder, it is there to be freeing. If one lives by the Word of God, so many problems can be avoided, but that is another devotional.

The Bible tells us in Jeremiah 29:11 NLT, "'For I know the plans I have for you,' says the Lord. 'They are plans for good and not for evil, to give you a future and a hope.'"

Today we are going to see how the promises contained throughout the Bible can free a person from the bondages that are plaguing their hearts, bodies, and minds. I can tell you firsthand, these bondages can tear you apart.

When I was younger, I did not realize my worth. I was very insecure. I looked for love and fulfillment in success, relationships, and responsibilities. Although I had a foundation in the things of God, I was not living for God. I was living for me and ignoring the leadings of the Holy Spirit.

Throughout the trials and tribulations I have faced, I have learned that only God can truly fulfill me. I have walked through the depths of depression and soared on the heights of personal success. I have had good and bad relationships, both personally and professionally. Nothing I have ever gone through can compare to the

The First 30 Days

promises I know I have in Jesus. These promises remind me that I can live a more victorious life.

The Bible says in 2 Peter 1:3-4 NIV, "His divine power has given us everything we need for a godly life through our knowledge of him who called us by his own glory and goodness. Through these, he has given us his very great and precious promises, so that through them you may participate in the divine nature, having escaped the corruption in the world caused by evil desires."

Many things that plague us are caused by what the Bible calls "evil desires." In and of themselves, they do not seem harmful, but taken to the extreme, anything can get you off balance.

For example, a workaholic can justify their desire to work because they provide a lifestyle they and their family desire. But working too much can turn into a detriment in the workaholic, hindering both their time with their family and time with God the Father.

Likewise, addictions of any kind can cause our balance in life to tip negatively. Many people get addicted to sex, gambling, drugs, alcohol, pornography, hobbies, and even power and control, among others. They allow these addictions to take center stage in their lives. They place them where God is supposed to be, thus creating an imbalance.

The Word of God is there to bring balance to our lives that we cannot find elsewhere. The Word of God is the great scale against which we can measure our lives. When your weight starts to tip to one side, He draws you back in. He gives you promises to stand on! (Matthew 11:28-30 NIV; Proverbs 3:5-6 NIV)

Stress/Anxiety – 1 Peter 5:7 NIV, Psalm 94:19 NIV, Proverb 12:25 NIV, Ecclesiastes 11:10 NIV, Philippians 4:6-7 NIV,

Needs – Philippians 4:19 NIV, Philippians 4:6-7 NIV, Isaiah 43:19 NIV, Isaiah 54:17 NIV

Addiction – Corinthians 10:13 NIV, Corinthians 6:12 NIV, Corinthians 15:33 NIV, James 5:15-16 NIV, Romans 5:3-5 NIV

Grief – John 16:22 NIV, Revelations 21:4 NIV, Romans 12:2 NIV, Psalm 34:18 NIV, Psalm 147:3 NIV, 1 Thessalonians 4:13-18 NIV

Weakness – Nahum 1:7 NIV, Psalm 73:26 NIV, Isaiah 54:17 NIV, Proverb 18:10 NIV, Philippians 4:13 NIV, Psalm 27:14 NIV

Confusion – John 14:27 NIV, Proverb 3:5 NIV, Psalm 143:8 NIV, 1 Corinthians 14:33 NIV, 2 Timothy 1:7 NIV

Fear – Proverbs 1:33 NIV, Joshua 1:9 NIV, Romans 8:31 NIV, Isaiah 54:17 NIV 1 John 4:18 NIV, Proverb 18:10 NIV

Troubles – James 1:12 NIV, Psalm 34:17-20 NIV, 2 Peter 2:9 NIV, John 14:1-31 NIV, Psalm 91:1-16 NIV, Luke 17:1 NIV

These topics and so many more are covered in the Word of God. All we need to do is take hold of these promises, do what the Word says, and enjoy the life that God wants us to have, a life of victory and success, not turmoil and destruction.

Verses to Ponder:

And whatever you ask in prayer, you will receive, if you have faith. Matthew 21:22 ESV

Ask, and it will be given to you; seek, and you will find; knock, and it will be opened to you. Matthew 7:7 ESV

Behold, God is my helper; the Lord is the upholder of my life. Psalm 54:4 ESV

But seek first the kingdom of God and his righteousness, and all these things will be added to you. Matthew 6:33 ESV

For the LORD God is a sun and shield; the LORD bestows favor and honor. No good thing does he withhold from those who walk uprightly. Psalm 84:11 ESV

Blessed be the God and Father of our Lord Jesus Christ, who has blessed us in Christ with every spiritual blessing in the heavenly places... Ephesians 1:3 ESV

He who did not spare his own Son but gave him up for us all, how will he not also with him graciously give us all things? Romans 8:32 ESV

Day 29

Who Will Never Leave?

BEFORE READING　　AFTER READING

Never Leave

Throughout my life, I have faced many trials and tribulations, some of my own making and some forced upon me by other people's choices. Looking back, I can see the hand of God as it has protected me, carried me, and guided me, in spite of my shortcomings.

The Bible tells us in Deuteronomy 31:6 NIV, "Be strong and courageous. Do not be afraid or terrified because of them, for the Lord your God goes with you; he will never leave you nor forsake you."

The saying, "Hindsight is 20/20," is so true. There were times, as I was walking through a valley, I could not see God working in my life. It wasn't until I had a clear view in the rearview mirror that I understood what God had done for me.

I look back over my life and I can vividly remember times that could have turned out much worse, but God was there to protect me. I often marvel at these times. God could have turned His back on me just as I had done to Him, but He did not. No, He was right there protecting me, in spite of my bad choices. This fact alone is an excellent testament to the love He possesses for each one of us. He chooses to love and protect us even when we reject Him.

This is because God's love is not conditional. God loves us despite our transgressions. The Bible tells us in Jeremiah 31:3 NIV, "The LORD appeared to us in the past, saying: 'I have loved you with an everlasting love; I have drawn you with unfailing kindness.'"

God does not love the same way humans love. He loves with a pure love that enables Him to love us in spite of our circumstances. This love means He will never leave or forsake us. Even if we walk away from Him, He will be waiting to welcome us back with open arms, just like the father of the prodigal son did in Luke.

See, God loves us so much that He will restrain His anger to give us a chance to repent. He is not waiting for us to make a mistake so He can strike us. No, He does the complete opposite. He waits as long as He can for us to repent. Nehemiah 9:17 NIV shows His love and compassion, "They refused to listen and failed to remember the miracles you performed among them. They became stiff-necked and, in their rebellion, appointed a leader in order to return to their slavery. But you are a forgiving God, gracious and compassionate, slow to anger and abounding in love. Therefore, you did not desert them,"

Although God's people had failed Him, He still forgave them for their sin. He did not give them the punishment they deserved. How amazing is it that we have a God who will never leave us and will always forgive us?

Verses to Ponder:

For the LORD will not forsake his people; he will not abandon his heritage;.. Psalm 94:14 ESV

It is the LORD who goes before you. He will be with you; he will not leave you or forsake you. Do not fear or be dismayed. Deuteronomy 31:8 ESV

Keep your life free from love of money, and be content with what you have, for he has said, 'I will never leave

you nor forsake you.' Hebrews 13:5 ESV

No man shall be able to stand before you all the days of your life. Just as I was with Moses, so I will be with you. I will not leave you or forsake you. Joshua 1:5 ESV

Day 30

Are You Living Successfully?

BEFORE READING | **AFTER READING**

What does living successfully mean to you?	What does Luke 16:10 mean to you?
Before reading, I feel...	After reading, I feel...
What three words do you think of when I mention God and Jesus?	Have you accepted Jesus as your Lord and Savior? If so, are you known by your fruits? If not, do you want to live successfully in Christ?

Salvation and Success

Although God is a forgiving father who wishes no one should perish (2 Peter 3:9 NIV), He is also true to His Word, and in His Word, He gives us clear instructions to come to know Him.

The truth is, we cannot walk in the promises of God if we do not have a relationship with Him. Note, I did not say *unless* we are saved. Salvation is the only way to eternal life. A relationship with God is the way to a successful life here on Earth. Therefore, you must have salvation and relationship to live a successful life.

So, what is salvation?

The Bible tells us in Romans 10:9-10 NIV, "If you declare with your mouth, "Jesus is Lord," and believe in your heart that God raised him from the dead, you will be saved. For it is with your heart that you believe and are justified, and it is with your mouth that you profess your faith and are saved."

In order to be saved from our sins, we have to both believe and confess that Jesus, the One True Son of God, was born of a virgin, came to this world, lived a sin-free life, and died on the cross to save us from an eternity disconnected from God. Once we do that, all God's promises are at our disposal.

So, how do we activate the promises of God after we have been saved and truly believe? First, we must have faith. The Bible tells us, "Now faith is the substance of things hoped for, the evidence of things not seen." (Hebrews 11:1 NKJV) You must use your faith.

In order to use your faith, you must know what the Word of God says. Thus, you must be in the Word. You must read your Bible and attend church. Learning the Word is like learning anything else in your life; you have to put time into the process of learning. You cannot set your closed Bible on the table and expect to gain all of God's insights. No, you must open it, read the words on the pages, and then digest them. You must attend a God-fearing, Bible-believing church that brings its body the Word of God, even when it is not popular.

Although knowing the Word is an amazing place to start, it is not the only requirement. See, many people know the Word of God, but they have failed to activate its power in their lives. To activate this power, you must do something with it.

The Bible tells us, "But be doers of the Word, and not hearers only, deceiving yourselves. For if anyone is a hearer of the Word and not a doer, he is like a man observing his natural face in a mirror; for he observes himself, goes away, and immediately forgets what kind of man he was. But he who looks into the perfect law of liberty and continues *in it,* and is not a forgetful hearer but a doer of the work, this one will be blessed in what he does." (James 1:22-25 ESV)

The Word is like electricity to our faith. Once we plug our faith into the wall socket of the Word, we have an unlimited supply of power. In fact, the Bible tells us we can do all things in Christ. (Philippians 4:13 NIV)

Peter Parker, better known as Spider-Man, coined the phrase,"With great power comes great responsibility." This is true in our faith walk. In order to live in the fullness of God's plan for our lives, we must be responsible for what He has entrusted to us.

The First 30 Days

The Bible tells us, "Whoever can be trusted with very little can also be trusted with much, and whoever is dishonest with very little will also be dishonest with much." (Luke 16:10 NIV)

God is not a person who will set us up for failure. He is a gracious God who has given us the Holy Spirit to guide our path. Then, at the right time, we will be rewarded.

To walk in the fullness of our faith, we must be willing to walk in God's commands, do the work required, and let Him guide us. We cannot live our life for this world and expect God to bless us. If we, as believers, are not living as the Bible commands, our faith will be hindered.

The Bible tells us faith without works is dead. James 2:14-17 NKJV says it like this, " What *does it* profit, my brethren, if someone says he has faith but does not have works? Can faith save him? If a brother or sister is naked and destitute of daily food, and one of you says to them, "Depart in peace, be warmed and filled," but you do not give them the things which are needed for the body, what *does it* profit? Thus also faith by itself, if it does not have works, is dead."

The Bible also tells us that we will know a tree by its fruit. (Matthew 7:15-20 NIV) Likewise, you will know a believer by their fruit, their words, their actions, their deeds, and what they hold dear. See, to have the power of God, you must be connected to God. You must be working your faith. You must believe you can do all things through Christ.

Now, the only caveat is this: God can and will do miracles. He WILL NOT be placed in a box of our ideologies. There will be times when we are not working our faith properly, but we will receive from the Lord. Then there will be times when we are doing everything right, but we do not receive as we had hoped.

In these times, we must remember Isaiah 55:8-9 KJV, "For my thoughts are not your thoughts, neither are your ways my ways, saith the Lord. For as the heavens are higher than the Earth, so are my ways higher than your ways and my thoughts than your thoughts."

At times, faith is not easy. At times, faith can be tested. Faith is not a one-way ticket to anything and everything you want, right when you want it. No, faith is a growing process in your relationship with God the Father. Faith is a process that you grow and build over time. Faith is part of the salvation relationship that grows you and molds you into the person God wants you to be.

Verses to Ponder:

If you confess with your mouth that Jesus is Lord and believe in your heart that God raised him from the dead, you will be saved. Romans 10:9 NIV

For the wages of sin is death, but the gift of God is eternal life in Christ Jesus our Lord. Romans 6:23 NIV

Looking unto Jesus the author and finisher of our faith; who for the joy that was set before him endured the cross, despising the shame, and is set down at the right hand of the throne of God. Hebrews 12:2 KJV

so that you might live in a manner worthy of the Lord

*and be fully pleasing to him as you bear fruit while doing all kinds of good things and growing in the full knowledge of God. You are being strengthened with all power according to his glorious might,
so that you might patiently endure everything with joy.*
Colossians 1:10-11 ESV

If we confess our sins, he is faithful and just and will forgive us our sins and cleanse us from all unrighteousness. 1 John 1:9 NKJV

For we are his workmanship, created in Christ Jesus for good works, which God prepared beforehand, that we should walk in them. Ephesians 2:10 ESV

For in the gospel the righteousness of God is revealed—a righteousness that is by faith from first to last, just as it is written: "The righteous will live by faith."
Romans 1:17 NIV

Eternal Choices: What Do You Choose?

ETERNAL CHOICES | REAFFIRMATION

Today I choose to...

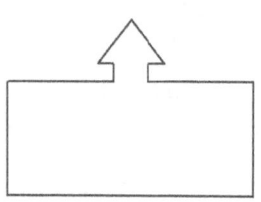

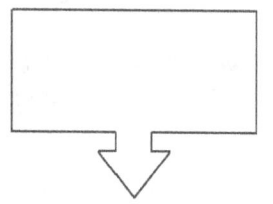

Today I choose to....

Today, if you accepted Jesus as your Lord and Savior, remember you will still have troubles, but you now have the power and promises to back you up. With the power of God, you will be able to handle any situation you face, but you will have to be an active participant. Faith is not a one-way ticket to easy street. No, it is a one-way ticket to Heaven and to a powerful life here on earth. Read, pray, study, and enjoy!	Reaffirming your devotion to God can be hard. It is easy to reaffirm your love when you are on an emotional high from spending time with God. The real test comes after the emotional high wears off, and you are in the middle of a trial. It is then you must remember the commitment you made today. It is then you will have your faith tested. Stand strong. My favorite verse says it best. Look it up. 1 Timothy 6:12 NIV

Eternal Choices:

Like everything else in life, you have a choice. You can choose to live in God's power, or you can choose to live in your own power. The first step is Salvation.

Salvation is more than believing there is a God. James 2:19 NIV tells us, "You believe that there is one God. Good! Even the demons believe that-and shudder."

Once you believe, you must also depend on and work with God to create a better life for yourself. You must seek a deeper relationship with Him, one that will cause you to transform your life. The Bible tells us in 2 Corinthians 5:17 NIV, "Therefore, if anyone is in Christ, the new creation has come: The old has gone, the new is here!"

When we accept Christ, we become a new person, maybe not instantly, but over time we transform from glory to glory. Yet we have to make a conscious decision to follow Him. We can also choose to deny this gift. If we choose to deny Him, we are choosing to live disconnected from Christ.

Throughout this devotional, you have read many of the trials I have suffered. Through them all, I have grown closer to God. Through them all, my faith has been strengthened.

Today I ask, do you know God as your Lord and Savior? This is the first step to living a successful life in Him. If you have a desire to make Him your Lord, you can pray a simple prayer. There is no magic in the prayer. The magic is in your belief.

Father God,

I come to You as a sinner. I know that I am not whole without You. I believe that You sent your Son to be born of a virgin, live a sinless life, die on a cross, and rise in three days, all so I could live in eternity with You. I ask You into my heart and life right now. I ask that You complete me and show me the ways I need to change. I ask that You send the Holy Spirit to lead and guide me through the trials to come. I thank You for your love, grace, and mercy. I thank You for showing me the way and creating in me a new person.

Amen

Reaffirmation

Some of us have prayed a prayer similar to that one. We know God as our Lord and Savior, but we have not been walking in a way that is pleasing to Him. This is the time to study your heart and ask God to help you through your doubt and unbelief, your sin, or anything that has put a wedge between you and God. Now is the time to reaffirm your commitment to Him and begin to walk as God would have us walk. It is time for us to stop living for the things of this world and start living for the things of God.

The truth is, no one is perfect. We have all sinned. Some of us are better at hiding our sins from others,

The First 30 Days

but God sees all. We cannot fool Him. So why even try? Today is the day to reaffirm our dedication to God. Today is the day to make a conscious effort to choose Him, no matter what the circumstances may hold. Today is the day we put Him first in our life.

Father God,

I humbly come before You and ask You to forgive me of my sins. I ask that You show me Your will for my life. I ask that You lead me down the path of righteousness so that I may be pleasing to You. I pray that You give me the grace and power needed to turn my sins around and walk fully in Your light and Your love.

I pray I bear much fruit for the kingdom of God. I pray that when my time is up, I hear, "Well done good and faithful servant." I pray You refill me each day with the power of Your Holy Spirit and continue to guide my path.

Amen.

No matter which prayer you prayed, our God is faithful, and He will honor your desire to be closer to Him.

For my last words, though, I want you to know that there are good, God-fearing people who feel, or have felt, the same way you feel right now. Life can be tough with all the trials we face, but just as I have found, with God and the people He places in our lives, we can be successful.

Take time and ask God today to show you what part of

the body you are. Ask Him to line up your desires with His, and then step out in faith. You never know where He will lead you.

Love always,

Katina.

Verses to Ponder:

Fight the good fight of the faith. Take hold of the eternal life to which you were called and about which you made the good confession in the presence of many witnesses. 1 Timothy 6:12 NIV

God is our refuge and strength, an ever-present help in trouble. Therefore we will not fear, though the earth give way and the mountains fall into the heart of the sea, though its waters roar and foam and the mountains quake with their surging. Psalm 46:1-3 NIV

Surely God is my salvation; I will trust and not be afraid. The Lord, the Lord himself, is my strength and my defense; he has become my salvation. Isaiah 12:2 NIV

That is why, for Christ's sake, I delight in weaknesses, in insults, in hardships, in persecutions, in difficulties. For when I am weak, then I am strong. 2 Corinthians 12:10 NIV

New Book Coming Soon.....

His Blood, My Life

Read ahead for a taste of the author's upcoming immersive narrative book.

The day started with a simple text, "We can do anything you want today." As she lay there in bed reading her phone, she thought of how sweet that one text was. Not only had he let her sleep in, but now the entire day was at her fingertips. As she lay there, she thought about all of the things they would do together that summer. Although cancer had slowed him down, it had not dampened his spirit. It had, in fact, made him the husband that she had always wanted. From the moment he realized he was sick, he had become sweeter, more gentle, and loving. Where he once took life for granted, he started to tell those that he loved just how much he loved them. In the last year, he had truly become her best friend, thoughtful and kind.

Little did she know, as she lay there, that text would be the last text that she would ever receive from him. Had she known it would be her last day with him, she would have gotten up sooner. She would have held him a little tighter. She would have talked to him more instead of reading her silly book. If only she had known how badly the day would end, she would have changed so many things.

The First 30 Days

Unfortunately, she did not know what laid in store for her that day. So, consequently, she lay there enjoying the first few waking moments of her summer break. School was finally out, and the months of juggling chemo, radiation, doctors' visits, work, and a baby were finally over. Now, she could spend her time focusing on helping her husband beat the dreaded beast called cancer. Finally, she would be able to enjoy the family that they had made together.

As she lay there thinking about all they had endured, she heard her phone go off again. This time it was her mother inviting them to their campsite for the day. She slowly dragged herself from their bed and went to ask her husband what he wanted to do. Although she worried about spending the day so far from home, she agreed to go.

The hour drive was nothing out of the ordinary at first. She sat in her seat, determined to finish a book that summer. He drove and occasionally reached over to tenderly touch her hair. It barely registered to her that he was talking on his phone. She was deep inside her Christian romance novel when he began to speak to her. It took her a moment to realize that he was no longer talking on the phone, but instead, was talking to her. She put her book down and asked him what he had said.

"That was Ezzy," he replied. "He is a mess. They have sent his uncle home on hospice to die."

Then out of character, he turned from the steering wheel and looked her in the eyes. His piercing blue eyes bore a hole into her soul each time he looked at her. This time was no exception. The only difference was what he said caught her completely off guard, and she was not sure what to say.

"No one wants to hear that, Katina. No one wants to hear there is nothing more they can do for you." He said in a concerning tone.

That simple statement made her cringe. Was he talking about himself? Was he worried? As she wondered how ominous his thoughts were, the only words she could muster in response were, "I know. I can't imagine how everyone must be feeling right now." In the back of her mind, still full of faith, she was sure she would never hear the dreaded, "There is nothing more we can do." She was sure he would be healed, a wonderful testimony of God's power. So, as they drove the last few miles, she blocked out the conversation and her thoughts and focused on her book yet again.

Bibliography

Knowles, Victor (1998) "Promise and Fulfillment: Believing the Promises of God," Leaven: Vol. 6 : Iss. 3 , Article 4. Available at: https://digitalcommons.pepperdine.edu/leaven/vol6/iss3/4

ABOUT KHARIS PUBLISHING

KHARIS PUBLISHING is an independent, traditional publishing house with a core mission to publish impactful books, and channel proceeds into establishing mini-libraries or resource centers for orphanages in developing countries, so these kids will learn to read, dream, and grow. Every time you purchase a book from Kharis Publishing or partner as an author, you are helping give these kids an amazing opportunity to read, dream, and grow. Kharis Publishing is an imprint of Kharis Media LLC. Learn more at https://www.kharispublishing.com.

www.ingramcontent.com/pod-product-compliance
Lightning Source LLC
LaVergne TN
LVHW051523070426
835507LV00023B/3275